TRAVELLER

an autobiography by
Nan Joyce

Edited by
Anna Farmar

AL. Gulligan '86.

TRAVELLER

TRAVELLER

an autobiography by
Nan Joyce

Edited by
Anna Farmar

Gill and Macmillan

Published in Ireland by
Gill and Macmillan Ltd
Goldenbridge
Dublin
with associated companies in
Auckland, Dallas, Delhi, Hong Kong,
Johannesburg, Lagos, London, Manzini,
Melbourne, Nairobi, New York, Singapore,
Tokyo, Washington

7171 1388 4
Print origination by Keywrite, Dublin
Printed in Great Britain by
Richard Clay (The Chaucer Press) Ltd, Bungay, Suffolk.

The publishers wish to thank the following for permission to include copyright material in this book: Ewan MacColl and Topic Records for 'The Moving-on Song'. Every effort has been made to trace copyright holders, but if they have been inadvertently overlooked, they should get in touch with the publishers at the first opportunity.

For my mother
and
in memory of Róisín Farmar

Contents

Author's note	viii
1 A different-speaking people	1
2 Three sods of grass	14
3 As a traveller you don't have friends	22
4 The Bog Meadows	31
5 God's own children	41
6 A peculiar young fellow	51
7 No ring on my finger	58
8 Waiting for something better	71
9 Go! Move! Shift!	77
10 The will of God?	87
11 The chance to speak out	99
12 Arrest	111
13 A better understanding	117
Notes (All superior figures in the text refer to these notes.)	119

AUTHOR'S NOTE

It's an awful sad thing to have no education. If I knew how to write properly and had good spelling I wouldn't have done this book on tape. Anna Farmar recorded it and wrote it out for me — if I wrote a book by myself whoever published it would need a medal for bravery!

Nan Joyce

1.

A different-speaking people

My mother said
I never should
Play with the gypsies
In the wood.

If I did
She'd surely say
Naughty wan
To disobey.

When I was a child we were hunted from place to place and we never could have friends to be always going to school with. The little settled children would run past our camps — they were afeared of the travellers. Other people had a sort of romantic idea about us, because of the horses and the colourful wagons. They would ask us did we come from some place special like the gypsies that you see on the films. They thought that the travellers had no worries and that we didn't feel pain, or hunger or cold. The truth is that we're people like everybody else but we're a different-speaking people with our own traditions and our own way of life and this is the way we should be treated, like the Gaeltachts, not like dirt or drop-outs from the settled community.

Some of my ancestors went on the road in the Famine but more of them have been travelling for hundreds of years — we're not drop-outs like some people think. The travellers have been in Ireland since St Patrick's time, there's a lot of history behind them though there's not much written down — it's what you get from your grandfather and what he got from his grandfather.

The original travellers were tinsmiths and musicians and they were great carpenters, they made all their own musical instruments and the wagons and carts. Over the years they mixed in with travellers from other countries, like the Spanish who came to Ireland four or five hundred years ago. You can see the Spanish blood coming out today in our family; my mother and her brothers were completely dark. My mother's mother was from Roscrea, she was one of the Doyles and they're very dark beautiful people with big black eyes and shiny black hair.

My other granny's name was Power, that's a Norman name. Her people would have been English travellers who came here years and years ago and married in with the Irish travellers.

Then there were settled people who took to the road for various reasons and mixed in with the travellers. One of my great-grandfathers, going back six or seven grannies, was a Protestant minister. His son married in with the Joyces, a tribe from Galway. Other people were burned out during the Cromwell evictions or they were made homeless during the Famine. The travellers were used to coping with cold and hardship and hunger, they could survive anywhere because they had their own way of working and their own culture. But the settled people weren't used to managing on their own, they slept in old sheds and barns and did a sort of slave work on the farms. Some of them married in with travellers.

The various tribes have different beliefs and ways of going on. Some of them are strong fighting people because for hundreds of years they had to fight to survive, it wasn't that they were bad. You can tell what tribe a person is from by just looking at them. If I saw a group of travellers and there was one there from every part of the country I could pick out where each came from without even asking. The Wexford tribes are mostly red-haired and they have freckles though some of them are fair-haired. The Galway tribes are very dark and good-looking. My father's people, the O'Donoghues, came from County Longford and they had snow-white hair and very blue eyes and then there were Donoghues from Dublin who were very dark.

My father's name was John O'Donoghue and my mother's name was Nan McCann. They were married in 1937. I was born in 1940 in Clogheen, a little place not far from Ballyporeen in County Tipperary. My sister Kathleen is the oldest in the family, she's two years older than me, my brother Willie was born two years after me and the other children followed on like steps in stairs with just a year or so between them. I had eight or nine brothers and sisters.

John O'Donoghue—Sarah Power | Richard McCann—Nan Doyle

John O'Donoghue — Nan McCann

Kathleen **Nan** (Ann) Willie Chrissie Sally (Sarah) Paddy Michael Richard Peter Lily

When I was three or four we went down to Belfast to the Bog Meadows. It's a tiny place with little red-brick houses and a factory. All the wagons were piled in on top of one another and there was no privacy. Just like we are today we had no water or toilet. Even as a child I was the sort of person who could see what was going on; the way the travelling people were hunted from place to place and they never got to settle down.

Ireland was very poor then, especially the Free State, you couldn't get copper or brass or tin or anything like that so the travellers used to smuggle it in their wagons. They'd bring it into the Free State[1] in big hundredweight bales and they'd make tins and pots and lovely copper ornaments and buckets. In those days travellers were different; they were a very proud people with their own way of life that was precious to them. Some of them had to beg to survive but more of them could sell their wares and do various things to keep themselves going.

Some people gave us a welcome. If they were living on the side of a mountain, or in a real lonely place, they mightn't get to the town for six months and they loved to see the travellers coming so that they could get their pots and kettles mended and buy little things. In those days the half-doors would all be open. You'd look in across the door to ask the woman did she want anything and she'd ask you in to have a cup of tea. She'd say, 'Now, tell us all the news. What's happening in Belfast?'

So we were sort of newspapers and radio as well as everything else. And we were trusted: the woman of the house would go out the back or upstairs and she'd leave her money and know well no-one would touch it whereas today people are told to be afeared of the travellers.

In the summer we'd go travelling. We'd leave up the heavy wagons because it was easier on the horses, they just had to pull the car, and we'd sleep in tents. They were made from green covers with hazel branches for wattles. In the mornings we'd roll up the sides, and fold the bedding, fresh air would get in and the place would be cleaned up spotless.

Mother and Father had this thing for cleanness. Even though we only had an old wagon or tents in the summer everything had to be shining. The mugs might be washed perfectly clean but still a kettle of water would be boiled and thrown over them before Father would drink the tea. Mother was always bathing us and washing our hair. The old shampoo we had years ago was a powder and it had to be mixed with water. There was a picture of a lovely blondy-haired girl on the packet. Mother would mix the powder and water in a bottle and throw it on our heads. Our hair used to be glittering.

When we were leaving a camp Father would break so many pieces of thorny bushes and tie them together on the end of a long stick to make a broom and he'd sweep up all the camp. He'd even cover the marks of the fire with sods of grass so you'd never think there was anyone camping there. The only things left would be the marks of the horses: the ground would be trampled where they were tied.

I'm a free born man of the travelling people
Got no fixed address, with nomads I am numbered
Country lanes and byways were always my ways
I never fancied being lumbered.

Oh we knew the woods and all the resting places
And the small birds sang when winter time was over
Then we'd pack our load and be on the road
They were good old times for a rover.

There was open ground where a man could linger
Stay a week or two for time was not your master
Then away you'd jog with your horse and dog
Nice and easy, no need to go faster.

Downpatrick was a favourite place. We'd camp along by the lake and I'd go into the woods with my sisters to gather wild flowers.... It was like a paradise. Father used to go fishing for eels. When he took them out of the water they wouldn't die for a long time, if they were left down on the grass they'd crawl up along the wattles in the tent. When they were cooked they looked lovely and Father would say,

'Now, have some of them, they're very good for you,' and we'd say,

'No, those are the snakes St Patrick turned into the water!'

There was a big wood by the lake and we'd go out with baskets and collect hazel nuts. Around the camp fire at night we'd be cracking these nuts with our teeth. We all had great teeth because my father usen't allow us to eat sweets, he'd shout at us over it. He'd say, 'If you eat sweets now you'll have no teeth when you grow up.' He had lost two of his own front teeth in an accident and he made false ones out of old ivory buttons. He filed them down and polished them. He could take them out and put them back in again but they never used to fall out or slip up and down like false teeth. We didn't know about Father's teeth until I found them one morning a few weeks before he died. He took them from me: 'Oh, give them here till I throw them away.' We were afeared of things like that because travellers never used to have false teeth or glasses.

Downpatrick is a very old town, all on a hill. Father brought us in one day to show us the church, the place where St Patrick is supposed to be buried. It was a Sunday and we sat around the graveyard, my mother and all, and Father told us the history of St Patrick from a book he took out, and he sitting on one of the gravestones. He could read anything and he knew Irish and our own language that we've had for hundreds of years. Some of us call it *gammon* and more of us call it *cant* — it depends on which tribe you're from. It's a very old language, even older than Irish — some of the words come from the Bible.

When I would go out hawking with my mother she'd be selling things from the basket and she might say to me,

'*Gage* the *byor* for a few *collyins*,' that meant 'Ask the woman for a few potatoes.' Then she'd say, '*Gage* the *yorum*' and I'd ask the sup of milk. This was the way the language was used. When the police would come down to shift us or to hunt us on we'd say, 'Oh, the *wobs*, the *gammy wobs*.'

Coming along the road Father would tell us the history of all the places we passed through. I was always asking questions about old castles or houses or monuments. 'What's it there for? Who lived in it?' and Father would tell us. This was the way he used to teach us; if he'd been alive when we were older we'd all have been very well-educated.

My mother couldn't read or write, she never had any education and I think she felt a bit left out because my father was such a scholar. He would read medical books and if the children were sick he knew what to do. I felt sorry for my mother over that but of course my father used to read to her too and fill in the forms and do the letters.

Father was tall and handsome. He used to wear long riding boots and breeches with a yellow polo-neck jumper and he'd always have a whip in his hand. The way he dressed people never took him for a traveller but he used to make a point of telling them because he never was ashamed of it. He was a great man for dealing in horses and going to fairs. He would get in with settled people living in rich houses, advising them about horses if they had spavins or sand cracks.

In Cushendall Father would deal with the farmers. He'd buy untrained horses from them, two-year-olds. They were beautiful piebalds, really well-bred; you hardly ever see those kind of horses now. Father would spend weeks training them. He'd break a big piece off a bush and tie it on a rope. Then he'd make the horse pull it and trot up and down the road. He never used to hit a horse or let anyone be cruel to animals.

When the horses were trained he'd shoe them. He'd pare their hooves and redden the horseshoe in the fire. Steam and smoke would come out when he put the shoe on the hoof but it didn't hurt the horse. I used to love the smell of the horse's hooves scorching and we used to pick up all the little bits Father had pared off. In the summer evenings he would groom the horses, he would curry-comb them and plait their tails — he would even shampoo them and they would glitter like silk.

Father wouldn't have a mongrel dog, he used to breed little pedigree dogs. He had two little Yorkshires, a bitch and a dog and the bitch got into pup. Father was looking after it better than a young child and when he'd be going anywhere he'd tell my mother to mind it.

One evening he went off to the horses and the little bitch had her pups and didn't she eat them! A full-bred little dog will eat the first pups, you have to watch them. My father went mad

My father

My mother

Father and mother together

Kathleen

Willie

My sister Chrissie Ward with her daughter

My daughter, with some of her small children, making a point that people often forget

DEREK SPEIRS (REPORT)

Talking to a journalist outside my front door during an election campaign over them, he nearly cried. Mother wasn't interested, she had no time because she was always washing and cleaning. She used to bake lovely bread; our oven was a pot with a lid on it and we had a skillet pot and a griddle. Sometimes when she was baking we'd come up and pinch a piece of bread unbeknownst to her and run away with it.

When I was young I was very thin, just straight down like a match but the go at the time was to be strong and well-made, the travellers thought a nice good-looking woman should be full-bodied. I was getting all kinds of things to feed me up; Mother used to give me malt, it was real thick and she'd spoon it into me. Then Father bought a big milking goat; a lot of travellers kept them and poor settled people, too, who couldn't afford to buy cow's milk.

Father would milk the goat every morning into cans that he made himself. He'd give us a mug of milk to drink and it would be hot! I never even liked goats, just to look at one turns me off and here I was drinking its milk. When Father went off I would get sick but he didn't realise this. He'd say, 'You'll be a great strong girl when you grow up, great hair and teeth and legs,' as if it was a pony he was talking about!

We were camping in the Glens of Antrim and one day Father and Mother went off to Belfast to buy swag. Swag is stuff to sell like scrubbing brushes or razor blades or leather thongs for boots. When they were gone Kathleen and Willie yoked the pony and car. The three of us lifted the goat up into the car and drove off about five or six miles to where there were sheep on a mountain and we let the goat go. When Father came back he went whistling down the road with the can and we were in an awful state over what we had done. Father looked everywhere for the goat, he thought it had just strayed and would come back in the morning. The next day he started looking for it again. He knew there was something wrong because this goat had got used to the place, the way goats are they're always eating around the fire.

Now we hated the camp we were in, there were trees growing over the road and it was lonesome but my father liked it and he wanted to stay for a while. He said to my mother, 'The goat is gone and I'm not leaving until I get it.'

When we heard this we nearly died with the shock, we said, 'Oh, God, he won't leave the camp at all now.' We were there for weeks. Every morning the children who had to walk miles to school would be passing and Father would ask them, 'Did you see e'er a little milking goat up the road?' and the children would say No.

One day a farmer came along driving a tractor and Father started chatting him, he used to get on very well with settled people. So he asked the farmer did he see the goat. 'Oh, yes,' said the farmer, 'there's a great milking goat up in the mountain, it's a piebald goat and it's in with my sheep and I wondered where it came out of.' So father went down and got the goat.

When we were in a lonely camp like that we'd be dying to move. Sometimes, if Father wouldn't shift we'd go up the road, open the gate and hush the farmer's cattle out on the road. (Of course, there was very little traffic at that time.) Father would get the blame, the police would come down and we'd be shifted.

On his chest Father had a tattoo of a beautiful Irish colleen. She had a green scarf and a black shawl and she always reminded me of my mother because my mother was very beautiful.

When we were in the country father used to go to bed very early and he'd lie back reading. His bed was at the door of the tent and Mother's was next to his, the boys had their tent for sleeping and the girls had theirs. Father liked to have a smoke before going to sleep so when he'd finished reading he'd ask my brother Willie to hand him in a light. Willie would get a little ember out of the fire with a spoon and hand it in to Father. Father would light a cigarette and give back the ember to Willie to throw on the fire.

One night whatever happened Father went to sleep without having a smoke. Willie had got so used to giving him the light that he got up in his sleep, took a little coal from the fire and handed it in to Father. The ember fell on to his chest and he jumped up but he didn't know what had happened.

Next morning when Father got up he took off his shirt to have a good wash. He looked in the mirror while he was shaving and he saw a big burn on top of the Irish colleen's nose! He called over my mother. 'Come here, Nan, till you see what happened.' He wasn't worried about his chest but he was sad about the colleen 'Look at the lovely Irish colleen — her nose is ruined.' You'd think she was a real person. Ever after when Father took off his shirt he would see the little mark on the colleen's nose and we would all go laughing, especially my mother: she was a very funny woman, always happy and laughing.

In the old thatched houses years ago crickets used to live in around the fireplace and you could hear them make a noise all night something like a clock. Father decided he wanted to have some for the wagon so he went off on his bike one day to an old man he knew who lived in a thatched house. The old man showed him the crickets and he put some in a matchbox — he made little holes in it for air. He brought them back to my mother but she was afeared of her life of them in case they'd go into the children's ears or their mouths.

Father gave Willie the matchbox to hold while he went into the wagon to find a place to put the crickets. Willie heard all the little scrapings within the box so he had to open it to see what was making the noise. All the crickets jumped out! Willie shut the box real quick. Then Father called him, 'Give me in the box now, son, I'll put them in the corner because they're supposed to love heat.' When he opened the box he said to my mother, 'That's the funniest thing I ever seen in my life.' Mother said, 'What?' She knew well what had happened and she was glad to see the crickets go — 'What's that, John?' Father said, 'I put four crickets into that box in the old man's house and now they're gone.' We all started laughing.

2.

Three sods of grass

Now and then you'd meet up with other travellers
Hear the news or else swop family information
At the country fairs we'd be meeting there
All the people of the travelling nation.

Oh I've kent life hard and I've kent it easy
And I've cursed the life when winter days was dawning
But I've danced and sang through the hale nicht lang
Seeing the summer sunrise in the morning.

I've made willow creels and heather besoms
Lifted tatties, pulled at berries and did hawking
And I've lain there spent, haped up in the tent
And I've listened to the old folks talking.

All you free born men of the travelling people
Every tinker, rolling stone and gypsy rover
Winds of change are blowing, old ways are going
Your travelling days will soon be over.

Fair day was a great time for all the travellers. We'd put in to a big fair green and the ponies, carts and wagons would be all lined up in rows. We'd be left at that time for we wouldn't be shifted on fair day.

The men would be swopping and dealing, some of them would have rotten wagons all painted up and others would have new ones, some would have real bad ponies and others good horses. When the swopping was all over they would go to the pub for their drink. If they got too drunk the men who had the new wagons might end up with the rotten ones, and maybe a man with lovely horses would end up after the dealing with two or three real bad ones. But they usen't to worry about it because the next time at the fair they'd be a lot wiser.

The women would put on their best clothes for the fair, new skirts and rugs, and they'd all gather round cooking and washing. At that time they had no cots or prams so they would take down the collar of the horse's harness, turn it upside down and cover it with a rug. The child would be put sitting down inside the collar and it couldn't get out so it would be left there until the cooking and cleaning were all done.

The little boys and girls would be running around barefoot, their eyes lit up with excitement because if you were a travelling child you'd have no children to play with, just your own family, for months. They wouldn't have seen their friends for a long time and they knew they wouldn't see them again for a year.

The girls that time wore shawls and long skirts and all you could see was their faces. They never showed any parts of their bodies. When they'd take off their shawls to wash themselves their lovely hair would be all hanging around — they never used to cut it.

When the dealing was over there'd be a big camp fire in the middle of the field and the men would gather round and start drinking. There'd be music and singing and storytelling till morning.

A boy might meet a girl at a fair and fall in love with her and he'd be trying to ask her father could he marry her. If he didn't ask for her now maybe he wouldn't see her again for a year and then she might be married to somebody else. He would sit beside her father and maybe he'd be a large rough man and the boy would be half-afeared of him. He'd be handing him the drink and cigarettes to coax him up.

The girl would be ogling the boy from behind her shawl and she'd be saying, 'Ask him now, ask him now,' because her father might be in good humour when he was drunk. The boy would edge up and ask him and maybe the father would give her but if he was a real contrary fella it'd be 'Get off outa that!' — he wouldn't give her.

In those days boys and girls didn't go out together. Even if they were allowed in to places as travellers, their parents wouldn't have let them go to a dance or to the pictures on their own, they always had chaperones, especially the girls. If you were a girl you were never really free because you were always helping your mother with the children. Since you were nine or ten you were holding the youngest child in your arms, you were sort of weighed down with them. You were never allowed go anywhere but when I was growing up we never just thought about it.

When the women were parting after the fair they'd swap shawls with one another as a gift. They'd all have had new shawls for the fair and they'd say 'Now there's mine for a keepsake.'

We used to go to a lot of fairs, and it really hurt me when I saw on the television a while back that the travellers weren't allowed into the fair at Ballinasloe. And they were the ones who started the fairs! My grandfather often told me that years ago the travellers started the fairs by bringing asses and goats to trade — they hadn't even got horses.

After the travelling men had been drinking all they would take was a thing we called 'greasy water'. It's made by boiling up a piece of lean bacon with an onion. The men thought this cured them, they wouldn't have tea or anything to eat. Now if you have a pain in your head you go for pills and tablets, the people have themselves poisoned, but years ago we had all our own cures. We'd make barley water for kidney infections and we had a salt cure for sore throats. You put a packet of salt in a saucepan and make it very hot. Then you empty it into a woman's nylon stocking and let it cool a little but not too much. Then you tie it round your throat and there's something in the salt that cures tonsillitis.

There were loads of cures for warts and they really worked. One used red matches: you wet a match and rub it on the wart three times a day for a week and then the wart suddenly disappears, the sulphur eats it away. Another one for warts used forge water. When the blacksmith was shoeing horses he'd take the red-hot horseshoe out of the fire with pincers and he'd dip it into a barrel of water to cool it. The barrel would be there for maybe a year with the blacksmith using it every day. If you had warts on your hand you dipped it into the forge water.

It was a sort of a healing thing too because with a lot of the cures there was a prayer, either the Sign of the Cross or the Hail Mary.

My father used to buy yellow sulphur in the chemists and he'd give us half-a teaspoon in a cup of milk about every two weeks. It felt like sea sand in your mouth and it was supposed to purify your blood. I don't know whether Father was wrong or right but we never got hives or scabs or rashes.

If one of the children got a chest infection my mother would get red flannel, brown paper and a piece of lard. She'd hold the brown paper to the fire until it was real hot and then she'd rub the lard into it. She'd cut the red flannel the same size as the paper, put the two together and put it on the child's chest. It was a bit smelly but it really worked!

When we were cleaning our teeth we used the ashes from the stick fire — it had to be stick, you couldn't use coal or turf ash. When you rub it in your fingers the ash is like silk. You put it on a damp toothbrush and clean your teeth; it's dirty at the time but when you rinse your mouth out with water your teeth are snow-white.

If you want to have nice hair you boil some elderberries in a saucepan, then you strain the water and mix it in with some olive oil. An hour before you wash your hair you warm a spoonful of this mixture and rub it into your hair. Then you warm a towel at the fire and wrap it round your head. When you wash your hair it's like silk.

I had a sort of runny ear when I was a child. It was digusting and my mother had me to doctors and all but there was nothing they could do. My father got a cure from an old travelling woman. He took a piece of ash stick and put one end in the fire; the stick had to be green, not dry or rotten. When the heat got at the stick drops of water came out the other end, they weren't hot they were freezing cold, little drops with bubbles in them. Three drops were put in my ear so many times a week and it was completely cured.

Travellers had their own codes too. If a group of them were coming along the road some of them would have better horses than the others and the one with the lazy horse would be left behind. Since a lot of the travellers didn't know how to read, a signpost was no use to them for telling them where to go. The group who came to the main road first would pull three sods of grass — and the sods had to have plenty of mud on them — and they would throw them on the road in the direction they were going. The sods wouldn't blow away and if a car drove over them they wouldn't go off the road for days. This was the travellers' signpost and the three sods of grass were the Father, the Son and the Holy Ghost because prayers came into everything.

When the men were drunk they might have a boxing match but they'd fall more times than they'd hit each other. Next morning they'd have a black eye each and they'd be ashamed to get out of bed to face each other. The women would be arguing with them over the way they were carrying on the night before. I often saw my father with black eyes. He'd be afeared to look out of the wagon in case some big man would walk up to him. He'd hold his hand over his eye and he'd say to my mother, 'Nan, who was I fighting with last night, did I do wrong?' and my mother would say, 'You did do wrong last night.' And then the two men that were boxing would shake hands — they never kept in any spite or hate. The first word in their mouths would be 'I'll never drink again, there's a curse over that drink and it's not lucky.'

Then the women would march them to the priest to take the pledge. This would be against their will but the women would go on, 'You're taking the pledge this morning because we're not going to stick it no longer.' If the men didn't go the women would tie their clothes in a bundle and leave them. So the men would be brought to the priest and they'd let on to be real innocent saying, 'Oh, Father, we didn't mean to fight.' They'd take the pledge for six months or a year and the women would have great peace then. They'd be all happy washing and cooking and making clothes for the children.

When the men had taken the pledge you'd see the change in them in a few days. Father would start to build a wagon. First he'd build the wheels, then he'd make the body and put the top on the wagon. He'd spend months carving the spindles for the back rack in the wagon; it's for holding all the spare stuff. He used a very thin, sharp knife called a peg knife.

Last of all he would paint the wagon. It was like something from *The Book of Kells*. Some of the drawings were of horses' heads and you'd think they were real because you could see the veins in their necks standing out. They would look really natural. When it was all finished Father would stand back and look at the wagon, it was so beautiful.

The travellers always loved to have nice wagons. I remember once when we were camping outside Purdysburn there were other travellers with us and one man had a beautiful wagon. He was aged about thirty and he wasn't married — this was a very old age for a traveller to be single because you were ancient if you got married at that age. Another man camping with us had an old rough wagon and he was dying to get this man to swop but he wouldn't.

Before they went to bed the travellers would sit around the fire to talk about ghosts, they had this thing about ghosts and the dead coming back. This man was afeared of his life of a ghost but he went off to bed in his beautiful wagon. He lay back in the top bed, it's like a bunk, having a smoke. He left the top half of the door open; you always have to do that because wagons are very stuffy.

The man who wanted to swop had a big greyhound. He got an old black shawl and tied it around the dog's shoulders and he tied an old cap on its head. Then he put its two front paws on the closed half of the door so it was looking in at the man smoking in bed. He saw the old cap and shawl and the greyhound looking straight at him and he thought it was a ghost! He squeezed himself out through the back window of the wagon and came running in to my father and mother asleep in the tent. He jumped in on top of my father and said, 'John Donoghue, John Donoghue, let me in, in the name of God and His Blessed Mother and I'll never stop praying for you!' So my father said, 'What's wrong with you? You're already in.' He said, 'I'm after seeing a ghost looking in over the door and it must have been my great-great-granny. I wouldn't mind if it had to be a nice-looking ghost but it was the ugliest ghost I ever seen!'

This was the trick the other man played on him the way he'd swop the wagon.

The wagons were part of the travellers' life but now you hardly ever see one. I can remember a few years back we thought we'd love to have a wagon, the way you long for old times that will never hardly come back. My husband bought a wagon and we said to our boys, young little ones they were then, 'Now, we'll make a bed in the wagon for you, won't it be lovely?' But when it was finished they wouldn't sleep in it! 'We're not going to sleep in that thing there,' they said, 'people making a laugh of us sleeping in a wagon.'

Some horses were good trotters and in the evening the men would yoke them and trot them up and down and bet on them. Other horses would be for pulling but there was always a favourite that you'd never sell or swap. We had a big piebald called Shirley; she would stand quiet and the children could walk under her legs. She was knocked down by a car once and got a terrible wound on her neck. Father sewed her up with a needle and catgut and she was as good as new.

Years ago the travelling men were always swopping or shoeing horses, or making tins, there was never a spare moment for them to sit down or think or worry. And they all knew how to play Irish music. On a summer's evening when the work was done and the tools put away they would all join in together to play Irish music and you would see children out dancing in their bare feet.

But that was in the summertime. In the winter it was awful because you couldn't sit outside. If you had a fire outside the front of you was warm but your back was completely freezing. In the wintertime we used to live in the wagons. We'd spend about six months travelling all round the North and then when the real bad weather came we'd go back to Belfast and we'd be hunted from one mucky field to another.

In the evenings the top half of the door would be open and the bottom half closed. The Tilley lamp would be hanging over the door so we'd have some light inside and outside. It would come time for the catechism, the penny catechism we used have years ago. My father would have a little sally rod about as thick as a match and he'd be waving it. It was springy and if you got it across the legs you'd really feel it. My father never battered us, he'd never hit us hard, but while he was teaching us the catechism we'd be looking at this sally rod, going.

Sometimes he'd call me 'little Nan' because my mother was Nan and when I was called she'd answer and when she was called I'd answer so he put little Nan on me. He'd say to me,

'Now, little Nan, who made the world?'

'God made the world, Father.'

'Where is God?'

'God is everywhere, Father.'

Then he'd go round and ask each of the children a different thing. The seven deadly sins: those were bet into our heads! We'd go real quick, 'Pride, coveteousness, gluttony, anger, lust, envy and sloth,' but the hardest thing we had was the ten commandments. We'd go along lovely until we'd come to the fifth or sixth commandment and we'd stop blank because we'd forgot all about it. And he'd make us go over and over the ten commandments until we had them by heart.

'And what do you say when you're passing a chapel?'

'Blessed be Jesus, I adore thee most holy sacrament of the altar.'

And then the prayers would start, the Hail Mary and the Our Father — the Lord's Prayer. In the wagon there was nothing only boards on the floor, there was no carpet and your two knees would be paining, and you'd be praying for him to stop. If he was tired he'd stop real early, he'd just go on for a few minutes, but if he wasn't he'd go on for hours.

After the prayers it'd be the ABCs. We used to call it the 'Alphabet'. And the alphabet was written in white chalk on a piece of cardboard inside the door of the caravan so it'd show up and the Tilley lamp would be giving great light. So Father would come along with the sally rod and he'd point out the letters. My sister Kathleen was the oldest and she would be first. She'd go real quick 'A, B, C, D, E,' and then it'd be my turn and I'd go real quick and then my brother Willie, he was two years younger than me, and he'd go real quick. 'Oh,' Father would say, 'that's very good, now say it backwards.' And when he'd go backwards we didn't know one thing and he'd keep us there.

This went on every night, we were learning. But my father died when we were very young and he didn't get much time to teach us.

3.

As a traveller you don't have friends

My granny was a tiny little woman. She had a grey bun of hair right up on the back of her head and she had the bluest eyes I've ever seen. When she was young she was very fair, just like my father.

My grandfather was in the 1914-18 war and he got a sort of a pension out of it. He and my granny had a house in County Longford. They used live in it for six months and then they'd spend six months on the road. Travellers won't stay in a house in the summer, they have to get out when they hear the wind calling them and the birds.

The house had a stone floor and an open fireplace. My granny always had two skillet pots hanging over the fire and no matter when you'd go in she'd be boiling soup in one and potatoes in their skins in the other. Sometimes she'd boil up yellow meal, Indian maize, and give it to us in a big bowl with stripes. There was a big white table that was scrubbed clean and a dresser with all the souvenirs her sons and daughters gave her from different parts of the world. We used to come up for a visit every year from Belfast and when I would go to wash the things on the dresser Granny would say 'Now don't touch that, *a grá*'[2] She was great sport and always in good humour.

Some of my uncles and aunts married settled people in England but they would come back every so often and when the big fire would be on they'd start the *céilí*[3] music. Every one of my uncles could play Irish music — on the tin whistle, the accordion, the pipes or the *bodhrán*[4] which they made out of goatskins.

Granny would sit on a stool by the fireplace and she'd start lilting 'Saddle the Pony' or 'The Longford Collector'. She'd have a clay pipe in her mouth and her foot would be keeping time to the music. My cousins were great dancers and when we came from Belfast Granny would say, 'Can you dance, *a grá?*' but we wouldn't, we never learned any Irish dances.

One summer when I was about nine years old we went off to Scotland. My sister Kathleen stayed behind with my granny and grandfather; since it was the summertime they were out travelling. We got the boat from Larne to Stranraer, that was the easiest way with the horses and wagons.

We travelled all of Scotland and it was a really beautiful country. We were left anywhere because there was just the one family of us in it. Tourists used to come and sit with us around the fire at night and Father would play the Irish music.

Other times we met in with the English travellers and we'd camp with the Romany gypsies. Father would deal with them and swap wagons or horses and he'd learn their language and they'd learn ours. There'd be a big fire at night and maybe ten families around it, cooking. All the children would be put away to bed and the prayers would be said. The men would sit around the fire and have a few drinks and then the women would gather round easy and there'd be music and singing and it was really great.

We went on down to England and stayed in Lancaster for a few months. It was a very nice place. Father was working on the building sites as a carpenter, he'd go off every morning with his tools.

I went to school in Lancaster and I found that the children and the teachers were so nice to me! They never once called me a bad name or anything though they knew I was a traveller. I really enjoyed going to the school there, the friends were so warm. What I remember most is the unusual names: we had a Thornyplum, Kathleen Winterbottom, Stuart Chalk. They were all high-up children from rich backgrounds, like doctors.

As a child I was delicate and one day I got sick in school. They had to send me home and all the little girls came with me, they caught me by the hand and brought me home to the camp. They used come up on Sundays and we'd sit down and play as children: I never met so many friends as we had there. As a traveller you don't have friends; you might have them for a little while but then you leave them all behind.

The police came and shifted us and I just hated leaving. We

were always aware that we were hunted, like rabbits, or like dogs after a fox, hunted from place to place. Maybe if we'd stayed there we'd have had an education. But of course, my father wouldn't stay that long in England. The travellers are peculiar people, although they were never really wanted in Ireland, they were outcasts in their own country still they had great love for it. When they were away the first place they would sing about was Ireland. No matter where they'd be it was always Irish songs and 'God bless Ireland' when they'd get drunk.

When we were in England or Scotland, we had an old wind-up gramophone — you were real rich years ago when you had one of them. One winter's evening, when the Tilley lamp was lit and the half-door was closed my father was playing a collection of Leo Rowsome, all those Irish airs. We were listening to the music when we heard a noise outside of nailed boots on the road. When the reel stopped, I think it was 'The Longford Collector', there was a shout in to my father

'Good man yourself! Play us another tune.'

My father looked out across the half-door and there was a farmer, about fifty years of age, down to do the Irish dancing. He thought my father had been playing the pipes. He said,

'That's the greatest music I heard for a long time — we used to dance at the cross-roads when I was a boy.' My father explained that it was records we had and he must have played them for over an hour.

As he was leaning across his bike the farmer was telling my father this sad story. He came from the West of Ireland and he was engaged to a lovely Irish girl but they were very poor so he went away to England to earn money to buy a bit of land. When he went back wasn't his girl married to someone else. When he was telling this story the tears were running out of his eyes about his girl. 'I came back here,' he said, 'and I never went back to Ireland again. I lost the only girl I ever loved.'

He came down the next morning when we were shifting and he said, 'If you're ever coming round here again you're always welcome to camp there and put your horses out on the land — don't be afeared to do it.' When we were going he kept looking after us; he was really a sad, lonely person.

When we were growing up we had this thing about cleanness

and if we were out in the day we wouldn't ask tea until we came to a real clean house. It was unusual for children but of course it was from our mother and father, always looking at them. If we saw a woman in a house with dirty nails or teeth we wouldn't ask her for tea. Willie would say to me in *cant*, 'Will we ask tea here?' and I'd say, 'No, Willie, we'll go to the next house, it might be cleaner.'

We'd never drink out of a stranger's cup and when the woman would be making us tea we'd say, 'Now put it in a bottle' — we thought it would be cleaner than cups because nobody ever drank out of the bottle.

Coming up to Christmas we met up with a travelling man and woman. The woman was sort of a hard case, some women are tidy and more of them are not. She was a lovely person but her nails were always black. On Christmas Eve we were all around the camp fire and she started making a Christmas pudding. She put in some stout and currants and raisins, everything that you put in a pudding, but she mixed it with her hands. She tied it in a clean white cloth from a flour bag — at that time everyone used flour bags, you'd get loads of them in the farmers' houses — put it in a pot of water and let it boil for so long. Then she took it out to cool and it turned out lovely.

The next evening we were all sitting around the fire. My father was dreading this pudding because he didn't want to hurt the woman's feelings by refusing it but he never would eat food that had been mixed by hand. She took out this pudding and put it on top of the grub box. We had no cupboards or presses or anything for holding the food so we had a grub box with a lid on it. It had a place for knives and forks made into it and a place for milk and other things. Every morning it would be scrubbed out with bleach, dried and the food put back into it. This was the only way we had of keeping the food together when we were travelling round.

The poor woman was a lovely person and great fun. She spread a white cloth on the grub box and put the Christmas pudding on it. My father was dying. He started scratching his head and he didn't know how to get away from the fire. She cut the pudding up and put it on plates and said to my father, 'Here, John, have a little bit of that, it's lovely.' Father didn't want to be ignorant,[5] to refuse it, but he had it in his hand on the plate, and he had it and had it. He was chatting away with this in his hand and he said to me, 'Here, little Nan, you eat that, it's lovely pudding.' 'No,' said the woman, 'I'll give Nan some.' 'No,' said Father, 'Nan'll have it.' She passed no remark, she didn't catch Father on and he didn't want to hurt her feelings.

I was the same sort as my father and mother, when you're brought up like this you can't help it. I was sitting at the fire and I kept looking at the plate. I was dying for a piece of pudding but I couldn't put a bit of it inside my mouth. I sort of moved away from the fire, reversing real easy with the plate in my hand until I got away. One of Father's horses was tied up behind the camp so I fed him the Christmas pudding.

Next morning the horse was very sick, it was all swollen up and I was full sure it was the pudding. I didn't know how to tell Father I was after poisoning the horse. Father got the vet and he said that the horse had eaten a poison tree — a yew tree — and if it wasn't seen to immediately it would swell up and die. When I heard what the vet said, I was really happy that it wasn't the Christmas pudding!

My father used to love stopping with this woman but when it came to making the tea you'd get away from the fire. Her husband was always telling jokes and stories; we had great crack years ago on winter's nights and summer's nights around the big fire outside. He told my father this story:

The travellers used to smuggle guns for the old IRA, because they were travellers they wouldn't be searched. One summer's day, when he and his wife were very young, soon after they were married, they were going along the road with their ass and cart looking for a camp. His wife was sitting up in the cart and they had guns hidden under the straw. Years ago the men never used to sit up, they always walked. Two Black and Tans came along and they were getting ready to search the cart. Someone had told them about the guns.

It was a real hot summer's day; the flies were gathered around the donkey and its tail kept swishing them away. The man said to his wife 'We have to make up a plan — if we don't we're finished, we'll end up our lives in jail.' He told his wife to start scratching. She didn't know what he meant and she didn't want to do it. He said 'Scratch, or we're done out of all our happiness — here come the Black and Tans to search us' so she started scratching.

He walked over to the two soldiers, scratching away, and he said to them 'Have you got any cure for lice, sir? I'm walking alive.' He pointed over to the ass, its tail swishing away the flies and he said 'Look at my old ass trying to beat them off and they're eating him alive.' When the Black and Tans heard this they backed away, they wouldn't come near him and they wouldn't go near the cart.

When the soldiers went off he lay down in the middle of the road, he was only young, and he cocked up his two legs jeering and he said to his wife 'Up Ireland, Mary, we won the battle that time!'

It was just like the smuggling years ago because in the Free State they hadn't really got a lot.

We travelled all over England and Scotland and got to know the names of so many places. We came to Gretna Green where boys and girls would go if they ran away together and wanted to get married quickly. Father showed us the big anvil they would hit with a hammer when they were getting married. There was a big old-fashioned coach there for visitors, it was there for hundreds of years. We all got into it, we were very small and we thought we were great, that we were in a cowboy picture. Father signed his name and Mother's in the visitors' book; I suppose they're still there. He used always do the unusual thing.

After about two years in England we took the boat back to Belfast; we always ended up there no matter where we came from because Belfast was like our home to us. Wherever you're reared you're always longing to go back there.

We hadn't seen my sister Kathleen all that time so we travelled down to County Longford, to Edgeworthstown where my granny lived. We used always camp in the same place on Mary's Road outside the town. A little girl came down on a bike: it was Kathleen but we didn't know her, we thought she was a settled child because she had her hair just clipped up behind her ears and traveller women and girls didn't cut their hair years ago, they kept it long. She was going up and down on her bike and she kept looking at us. I don't know if she knew us or not but we didn't know her because she had changed. She rode into the town and then my father went and brought her back. We thought she was awful looking! And she was so fat! My granny had been feeding her up.

None of our family was really fat but my granny was an awful woman for food. Even though you weren't hungry she'd say 'Come on now, *a grá*, eat it up, there's not a pick on you!' I was always skinny and Granny would say to my father 'Look at that little girl, *a garsún*,[6] do you not give her any food at all? She's starving.' She'd pull me over to her and she'd put her hand on my shoulders and feel the bones coming through. It wasn't because of the food, it was that I was born to be skinny; some women are born to be stout and more are born to be skinny and it doesn't matter what you eat it doesn't make any difference.

Granny said to my father, 'You're taking back Kathleen and you'll leave Ann for two years now.' Father didn't want to leave me because I was sort of the favourite in the family. But Granny said, 'Leave Ann here and we'll fatten her up and you won't know her when you come back.' She got around my father and they went off leaving me behind.

I nearly died in the house because I was a real traveller. I nearly faded, I got thinner and thinner instead of fatter. Every day I would open the door of the house and sit on the step. When the door was opened I felt I was free, that I could feel the wind beating in my face. Granny used to say 'Come in, *a grá*, and don't be sitting there and all the neighbours looking at you.' She would take me in and I would go upstairs in the little house and open the window and stick my head out!

My granny used to bake a lot and she would get big jars of malt — it was a great thing years ago with the travellers. She would spoon it into me, just like my mother, trying to put weight onto me, she was. She would come to me with a big bowl of soup, meaty soup that was all oily, and she would say, 'You won't know yourself, *a grá*, when your father comes back.' But instead of this making me stronger and fatter it was making me thinner because I was getting sick every night. My sister was able for it but I wasn't and then I was pining away to get off travelling. I loved to be out in the summer, to go among the butterflies and the wild roses. Sometimes I'd wear a little apron and fill it full of grasshoppers. Then I'd open the apron and they'd all hop out! We knew about the blackbird, the thrush, the cuckoo and the corncrake, everything that was wild we knew the name of it. I would love to be an artist, to paint all the things that are in my head, the beautiful places I've been to, watching Father down by the river grooming the horses and Mother baking bread at the camp fire.

After about two weeks my father and mother came back. 'We changed our minds,' they said, 'we won't leave Ann.' I was never as glad to see them! And Granny said, 'It's a good job you did come back or there would have been none of her there at all!'

Well, I was glad to get away but I loved my granny and grandfather. My grandfather was a quiet, gentle person. He didn't talk very much and he'd have to know you real well before he'd talk to you. He was always reading.

I'd like to settle in the winter-time
Away from the weather in a country town
But come the spring I'd get itchy feet
Then goodbye town and smokey street
I'd want to be moving some place else
So move along, get along, move along, get along
Go: move: shift.

We travelled down to Dublin and we were all delighted to have Kathleen back with us because we were great friends. We camped in Rathfarnham and I was getting ready for my First Communion and so was Willie, Kathleen got it with my granny. At that time travelling children were always in their bare feet they never had the price of shoes. A Protestant minister, I don't remember his name, used to go round the travelling people and buy the children shoes and socks. He and his wife would bring them all up to the shoe shop. It was really great of them. He bought us leather sandals with buckles and straps and he got me a pair of pink ankle socks. If he hadn't come along I'd have been in my bare feet getting my Communion!

The winter came. I hated it, I just couldn't bear the cold and the hardship. Now we have trailers and I know they're not much, they're freezing cold but at least we have them. But then we just had the roundy top wagon, barrel-tops they used to be called, and they're so small.

We all got the measles and we were very sick. My youngest

sister Sally was only two years old, we called her Sarah after my grandmother, she was a lovely little one. My mother put her into hospital. We were weeks sick but my mother cured us all and she was up and down to the hospital to see Sally. When we were better Mother took Sally's clothes and went to take her home. She came back with the little bundle and she was screaming. When she got to the hospital my little sister was dead. My mother couldn't believe it, it was impossible to believe. We never thought anything would happen Sarah on account of her being put into hospital. She was the youngest and we all thought the world about her. So she died and my mother never got over it because even to this day she speaks about it.

We stayed in Dublin and it was awful. The travellers were so poor they were reduced to begging but some of the Dublin settled people were very poor too. When the travellers went down the country they could make things and sell them, but we travelled back down to Belfast, we always came back to the Bog Meadows.

4.

The Bog Meadows

The people in the Bog Meadows were really lovely; they never called us 'dirty knackers' or anything like that. We were staying at the back doors of their houses with no water, no toilets, no bin collection, just like today, and still they didn't come out and call us names. They understood because they were poor oppressed people themselves.

Mrs McAloon was a settled woman who was very good to us. She lived in one of the little red-brick houses and she never refused us our water. We'd go in the back door to the kitchen and she'd say, 'Come on, bring in the bucket,' and we'd fill it up ourselves. There were bags of flour in the kitchen and this lovely smell of baking. When I'd go up for the water Mrs McAloon would say, 'Now, Ann, I have something for your tea,' and she'd give me out three or four hot apple tarts and a dozen soda farls. I'd take them home and put on the kettle and we'd gather round the fire outside and fill out for all the children.

There was another family called Cooke and my brother Willie used to go in and sit with them for hours. They were really dark and very beautiful like Spanish people. The father was a sweep. Willie would go in and sit and he'd forget to come home and my father and mother would be everywhere looking for him; if you were only missing for an hour years ago there'd be an SOS out for you. So my brother had this habit of straying off; if he wasn't in Cookes he'd be playing marbles with the little settled boys. Then my father would take the long trousers off him and he'd have to wear short trousers and this would keep him from roving.

Kathleen was missing one day and my father and mother were everywhere looking for her. They found her in the middle of the Corporation dump in Whiterock and every bit of her was covered in ashes. She was sitting there like a fairy reading *Dandys* and *Beanos* — that was how she learned to read, from the comics.

The little boys used to go to the dumps to look for bits of brass and scrap — I don't know what kept them from getting sickness. If one of them found a good patch he'd fill up his bag and then he'd say to the others, 'I got a lucky load — feel the weight of that!' And the other little fellow would say, 'Oh, why didn't you tell me before you had it all picked.'

In Belfast a lorry used to come every so often with big tubes and it would suck all the dirt out of the drains at the side of the road. They would empty out this thick black, oily stuff and we'd get a stick and poke in it for pennies and sixpences and maybe half-crowns. Our hands would be completely ruined with this oily muck. We'd bring the money home and get a bath of suddy water to wash it in. We'd have to scrub our hands too because there would be an awful smell off them.

When these lorries came around the Bog Meadows washing the paths and putting disinfectant down the drains my mother would run after them with a bucket and she'd say, 'Will you give me some of that for around the camps?' and they'd give her this black Jeyes Fluid and she'd mix it with water and clean around the camp.

One Twelfth of July I went down to Sandy Row with Willie and we were all day watching the Orangemen marching and listening to the music. I had a skipping rope and I'd go skipping along beside them while they were marching. The noise of the drums: some of them beat the drums with their hands and they got all sore.

When I told my father about it he nearly went mad; growing up we heard about the Orangemen being bad but they never did anything to us, I suppose they knew we were travellers the way we were dressed.

The Protestant side of the Bog Meadows had a bonfire and they got old trousers and a coat and hat and they set this thing alight. It was like a scarecrow and it was supposed to be the Pope. I thought it was really stupid, I'd say to my father and mother, 'How could that be the Pope — it's only old rags.'

Ever since I was little I hated begging; we never could beg in the street, we were always ashamed and sometimes when we'd go to a door the people would be as poor as ourselves. Travellers begging had to make themselves all miserable-looking before they'd be given anything but when you were selling something it was different, you felt better.

My father used to make flowers for us to sell from baskets. He would hold an elderflower into his knee and keep carving up and down with a sharp peg-knife and it would come into a beautiful flower. Then we'd dye them all pink and red and they were just like natural flowers — you hardly ever see them now. We used to make nylon flowers too.

I was supposed to be a great hawker when I was small because I could get round the women, I knew all the ladies in the big rich houses and they would keep clothes for me and bring me in. Often they would go out to get a cake or pastry for my tea and leave me in the house. When you didn't take anything people trusted you and you felt better, you always knew if you were trusted.

In the Lisburn Road there were two old ladies living in a great big mansion and I used to call on them. They were real respectable and had lovely talk. If I wasn't round in a month they'd be wondering what had happened to me. 'Oh, there you are Ann,' they'd say when I came. 'Where were you? Were you down to the country, were you down in Dublin?' This is why I love the old people because they were always very kind to us when we were growing up. These two ladies reminded me of two old film stars with their hair in big buns and gold earrings and jewellery on them. I used to tell them jokes and they'd be laughing their heads off.

They brought me upstairs one day and showed me an old-fashioned trunk with studs on it. It was full of beautiful dresses and hats. They gave me a little silver handbag with a chain, the kind posh people had years ago when they'd be going to a dance. Some of the hats were real wide with big roses on them. 'Now, keep them, Ann, till you grow up,' they said. 'They'll be lovely on you then, you have this lovely walk.' I was tall for my age and slim but I was a child, I didn't know what they were speaking about. They used to ask me, 'How did you learn to walk like that?'

It was my father taught me. If you were a girl you couldn't sit in a hunch or lie back, you always had to sit up straight and

DEREK SPEIRS (REPORT)

The travellers' official halting site at Belcamp, on the north side of Dublin

speak out straight. My sister Kathleen used to walk with her feet turned out and I walked with my toes turned in, so Father said to us one morning, 'Some day you'll grow up and you'll have to learn how to walk and how to sit right and I'm going to give you a lesson on how to walk.' He was a character sometimes, my mother used to break her heart laughing at him.

He got a dish of water and he made Kathleen walk with it on top of her head and Kathleen was afeared to stir in case the water would fall down on top of her. She had to walk with her neck real stiff and her head up in the air and then my lesson would come and I was afeared of the water. He'd say to Kathleen 'Your two feet are turning out, you can't walk like that, you must keep them straight.' And he'd keep at us. He got my sister walking straight and now today she has a lovely walk.

There was another big house in the Falls Road I used to go to. A very old lady lived there and she would bring me in and give me tea. I think she used to be lonely for she would keep me chatting for hours. 'Oh, haven't you a great life,' she would say. 'Look at the things you can learn, now, the way you live.' But little did she know the way we were living, if she did she wouldn't believe it.

Round her neck she wore three rows of amber beads, you had to put them on wire because they would eat away thread. I used to wear lots of bracelets and she'd say, 'Ann, some day I am going to give you a lovely present, and I want you to give it to your father or mother to put away for you when you grow up.'

She used to hate to see me going, she'd keep talking to me about where we travelled and where we lived. I'd tell her about my brothers and sisters — she couldn't believe I had so many! She must have had no family because there was no one in the house only herself.

I was going to her for years and sometimes I'd do little things for her, sweep the floor or wash the cups. One day she said, 'Ann, I have the present for you. I have it since I was a young girl and you must put it away, it's very precious.' She gave me a long box. I opened it and inside was old faded velvet — and the amber necklace from her neck. 'Promise me', she said, 'that you'll give that to your father or mother because it's very valuable.'

The necklace was beautiful but I didn't like it, it was for an old woman, it was too big for me. 'Always keep that,' she said, 'and remember me.' The strange thing was that when I went back to the house afterwards no-one ever came out to me. She must have died, she must have known she was going to die. I don't know what I did with the necklace: if I had it now I would never part with it.

When we were done hawking for the day we'd go through all the clothes we were given and pick out any that would fit us. We'd take the rest to the little houses in the Bog Meadows and sell them for a few shillings; the women would be grateful to see us coming. This would be more money for food.

We'd hide any money left over, we all had our favourite hiding places, maybe under a stone or a sod of grass. I'd hide my money for the pictures and Kathleen would have her little place and Willie had his. Willie started smoking and he had his five Woodbines hidden with his money. Kathleen would take a puff out of the Woodbines too and so would I — if Father had caught us he would have killed us! One day Willie came unbeknownst to us and he picked up my money and Kathleen's and his own and he went off spending it on candy apples and marbles and we were going to kill him. He said to Kathleen, 'If you hit me I'll tell my mammy that you're smoking!' So Kathleen couldn't say anything to him.

We used to save up to go to the pictures. In the back of one of the red-brick houses in a galvanised iron shed a man used to show black and white films on a tiny little screen, it was like a television. We used to pay sixpence, that was the old money, to get in. The three of us used to go and other little travelling children with no shoes on, their faces not washed. The women in the little houses used to make candy apples to earn a few shillings and we'd all have them and they'd stick in our hair. In the middle of Hopalong Cassidy or Roy Rogers, when we'd just be getting interested, the film would break down and we'd all boo. We'd roar at the man, 'Come on, now, give us back our sixpence — we've only seen half of it!' The noise of the children! Then he'd get it going again and we'd really get down to it. When we'd come out my brothers would let on to be Hopalong Cassidy with the horses.

When we had the money we'd go up to the Broadway. This was the big night out for us. We were always together, like the Three Stooges, I think it was because we got it so hard sometimes it brought us closer together. One film we saw in the Broadway was *Calamity Jane* with Doris Day. My sister Kathleen was a lovely girl and she was growing into a woman just like Doris Day; she used to wear jeans all the time, it was unusual for a girl in those days.

The travelling women years ago weren't really like settled women, they had all their own traditions. Sometimes if their husbands were drinking a few nights in a row they'd go off in a group looking for them and they'd search all the pubs in Belfast or Dublin. My father had a few favourite pubs in Belfast, one was in Smithfield and another one was the Beehive on the Falls Road.

One night when my father was gone out my mother said, 'I wonder what that fella's up to?' She put on his striped suit and his shirt and tie and even his boots, because my mother was a big woman, she took the same size of shoes as my father; he had very tiny feet although he was tall. She put on his topcoat, it was creamish coloured with a belt and leather buttons. Then she folded up her hair under his hat and she was just like Al Capone the way she was dressed! She got the bus down to Smithfield to the pub where Father used to chat with settled men and do horse-dealing.

In went my mother to the pub and she sat down facing my father with his clothes on her and his hat and he didn't know a bit of her. She sat there all night with the cigarette in her hand, she usen't to drink that time, staring at him to see what he was up to. All he was doing all night was chatting to the men about horses and swapping whips and bridles so she got fed up. It was only at the latter end when the pub was closing that she told him who she was! Ever since when my father would go to the pub he would keep an eye out to see who was sitting beside him.

The winter was terribly hard for the travellers and especially the women, trying to look after the children. Some doctors wouldn't bother with our children, they wouldn't come out to look at a traveller, so we had to bring the children in to the hospital on the Falls Road, they were good to the travelling people there. I found that the black doctors were the best, they were really kind and they understood us.

We used to be hunted out of the Bog Meadows. We'd go from the Catholic side to the Protestant side, then to the Falls Road, up to Andersonstown, out the Hollywood Road, up the Glengormley Road, the White Rock and the Show Road. We kept moving because we had to, there were big fines for camping. If you didn't shift you'd get a notice, a big form telling you what would happen if you didn't go. Then if you stayed they'd come out and and fine you, maybe £25 and that was an awful lot of money, you couldn't get it. If you didn't pay you had to go to prison. That was just for camping. Then you got more summonses for having no toilets, no water and this wasn't the travellers' fault.

You've got to move fast to keep up with the times
For these days a man cannae daunder
There's a bye-law to say you must be on your way
And another to say you can't wander.

Some of the police were very hard on us. They would come up at ten o'clock of a winter's night and it didn't matter if it was snowing or freezing the travellers would have to pack up. The women might have walked miles for two buckets of water to cook the food and wash the children. They might have spent an hour trying to light the fire. In the winter the sticks from the ditch are all wet and you can't get them lit. You'd be after throwing a bit of sugar on them to get them to light up at all hours of the night. The women would be trying to cook a bit of food for the children when the police would come and lift the bucket of water and throw it on top of the fire. It was the cruellest thing I ever saw.

Born at the back of a blackthorn hedge
When the white hoar frost lay all around
No Eastern kings came bearing gifts
Instead the order came to shift,
'You'd better got born in some place else,
So move along, get along, move along, get along,
Go: move: shift.'

We'd have to pack up everything in the middle of the night, and at that time we had no motor van or car, it was a horse and wagon. You couldn't say to the police that you weren't shifting because you'd be kicked around the road, the men would be beaten with batons, they'd even be brought into the barracks and locked up. You got no fair play at all if you were a traveller.

If you had any brain at all you knew that the travellers weren't wanted. Once in the North we stayed with two families for about a week, near Warrenpoint. One man's horse jumped through a gap into a farmer's field. A group of men came up about twelve o'clock of a winter's night with shotguns that they use for hunting foxes and rabbits. They shot this man in the legs and he was in terrible pain. We shifted but it was so dark we didn't knew where we were going. We camped at the edge of the seashore but we didn't know that the tide was going to come in so far and in the morning the sea was running around the tents.

We travelled around Portadown and Lurgan, to Ballymena and Newry, we travelled all of the North over and over again.

5.

God's own children

When my mother was expecting her last baby we were stopping in Whiterock in Belfast. She had to go into hospital because she wasn't keeping too well after having a big family.

My father went into town one morning to buy harness for a lovely little piebald pony he was training. It was a Friday and he brought back some fish and we cooked it. Next day he got up early and said, 'I'm going down the town today for I have to collect the bridle, the dealing man hadn't got it yesterday.'

Father used always come back at three o'clock at the latest when we were on our own but this day we waited and waited for him but there was no sign of him. He was the one for lighting the Tilley lamp in the evening when it got dark, because the lamp was dangerous, it would blaze up, and he was the one for turning it off at bedtime. When it got dark that evening we lit the lamp and put it hanging up in the roof of the wagon. Father had been reading to us from *Wuthering Heights*, I got it in Smithfield for a few pence. Every night he'd read us a chapter and we'd be waiting anxiously to hear the next bit but when he didn't come we put the wireless on and listened to 'Book at Bedtime' on the BBC.

There was a big deep quarry right beside our camp. About midnight, when we were in bed, we heard a man scream, like someone dying. My sister and myself and my brother heard it, the other little children were too young, they didn't understand anything. I said to Willie, 'We should go out quick, my father must be after falling down the quarry, he must have been killed.' But we didn't go out because we were afeared of the dark. And it wasn't my father: the time we heard the scream he was in the police barracks.

A very strange thing happened. After we heard the scream

someone came in the door. When you walk in a wagon the springs go down and the wagon shakes; we could feel the pressure on the door and the floor moving but we couldn't see anyone. We heard footsteps, the wagon went down a little bit — and the Tilley lamp was turned off.

Next morning the police came up and said Father was dead. He died in the police barracks. I never knew what happened; Father wasn't a man for going out breaking the law and he was a big strong man, very active. I don't know if my mother ever knew why he died but I was always thinking about the scream we heard at the same time Father was in the cell.

My mother had to come out of hospital and still my little sister wasn't born. Mother was in an awful state. She sold the horses to take Father's body back to Mullingar and she travelled the whole way with the hearse. She was about two or three days away, waiting until he was buried. We were left behind in Belfast on our own and we were in a dreadful state; we were so attached to Father and we'd think of all the things he used to do.

When my mother came back she had to go into hospital and a few days later my little sister Lily was born. There were nine of us children and the youngest were just a year older than one another. Kathleen was about fourteen, I was twelve and Willie was ten.

Years ago when someone died the travellers would burn whatever that person had; it came from the time of the plague, I think, but it's not done as much now. My mother burned the wagon; whatever we had, she burned it so we were left with nothing but she would rather it be gone than be looking at it because it reminded her and made her sad.

When I was emptying the caravan I found a book under Father's pillow; it was *Wuthering Heights* and he just had two chapters to go. I saw the film of it after and I thought of my father.

Some travellers won't stay where someone has died because it reminds them and they keep talking about it so we shifted from Whiterock down to the Bog Meadows and we put up a sort of a tent.

Everything was different after Father died. It was coming on to winter and life was getting very hard. We just had the tent and the few bedclothes, no shoes on our feet. I remember one time going out hawking with my little brother. My coat was too long for me and it was damp. It actually froze; it went as hard as a rock and when I was walking it rubbed up against the backs of my legs and they got all scalded from the hard, icy coat.

Kathleen and Willie and I would go to Smithfield and buy a few dozen *Old Moore's Almanacs* to sell. Sometimes we'd sell swag and then we'd bring the food home for my mother and the children. We knew every bit of Belfast, every corner and every street and what bus to get here and what bus to get there, we could get around it with our eyes closed. Some days my mother would go out to give us a rest.

I was always sort of psychic and I knew when something bad was going to happen. My mother got a summons for camping; it was for £25 and we couldn't pay it. When my father died, my mother never got a penny from any kind of welfare, no widow's pension, nothing. Now if you're stuck you'll get something, but if you don't know how to read and write how do you put in for these things, especially years ago. All mother used to get was the few pounds Family Allowance. That was the day she'd get something for the children, a few sweets or ribbons for our hair, she'd get some little thing for each one of us.

After she was summonsed my mother went off one night with another woman who had a pony and cart. They went off to steal scrap, bits of copper waste. It was the first time she ever did anything like this and she was caught. I know it was wrong but my mother was really a good person and this is how I know not to look down on people if they do something wrong. Good people can do something they'll be sorry about but if you're put in a corner and you have to do something it doesn't matter who you are you will do it. If you grow up rich you don't have to go out and steal.

Mother was arrested. She was kept in the police barracks and she never even got out on bail. She did a year in Armagh prison and that was a time of my life that I never forgot. I'm sure they must have known Mother had a large family but no-one ever came out to see did we need anything, were we on our own. My youngest sister was only a couple of months old and then my little brother was over a year and the other little fellow was over two, they were all like steps in stairs.

We left Belfast and went off travelling through the country with another family. We'd have been better off staying in the Bog Meadows because everyone knew us there and the other family had a lot of small children so we had to do everything for ourselves. Looking back now I don't know how we survived: God must have been always with us to mind us and look after us.

We had the loan of a white horse and a four-wheeler; there are sideways carts and flats and four-wheelers that you can build a wagon on but there was no wagon on this one. We used to camp about three miles outside Armagh and sometimes Kathleen would mind the children and I'd go hawking with Willie. I'd have the basket on one arm and my little sister on the other. I remember one freezing cold day going round the houses and my brother had no coat and he was in his bare feet. A woman followed us with a top coat for him and he put it on. It was miles too big, dragging on the ground but still he wore it because he was frozen and soaking wet.

When we went to Armagh we'd go to the prison. There was a little wall outside and we'd sit there for hours watching the warders go in and out. Sometimes women prisoners would be with them, doing the front garden and we'd look to see if my mother was with them. But we never did see her until the year was up.

When we were done hawking and dealing for the day we'd sit down on the path and count out the money we'd collected. We'd put the price of the milk on one side and the price of the bread and the tea and sugar and whatever else we could get. If we were short we'd start on again until we'd get enough and then we'd buy the few things and go home. And we were always in a hurry going back along if it was a winter's evening and turning dark. We grew up afeared of the dark and of strangers.

I was always the one that did the washing and the cooking where Kathleen looked after the horse and she got the sticks and built the tents, all those kind of things. We would make bread and milk, boiled milk and sugar. We'd start off with the youngest one, my little sister Lily, and we'd feed her till she was swelling, till she wasn't able to roar she'd be that full. And then we'd come on to the next one and we'd feed him up, we'd spoon this bread and milk into the three youngest ones so they'd be full up, there'd be no crying out of them. Then we'd start getting our own food ready. I don't know how the little ones survived, looking at the children today, the way they're looked after and the things they get.

The horse knew us like a bad ha'penny. He'd come up every morning to the fire to get yoked and we'd feed him with bread or whatever was left over. The four-wheeler was quite long, and we used to have all the children in the back with the blankets, they were like little chickens. Wherever we went they came. They were all real fair, you could see their hair a mile away.

Kathleen was the driver; her lovely blondey hair would be blowing and she'd be singing 'Whip crackaway! Whip crackaway!' to the horse. We called him King Billy's horse. She'd have the whip going and her two legs over the side of the cart and the horse would be going like the wind.

One day I never forgot: it was the first time Kathleen ever did anything like this. It wasn't raining, it was a sort of a dull day and as we were driving along we came to a house by the side of the road, a low two-story house with no garden. We knocked at the door but no-one came out so we looked in the bottom window. What was in the window for bad luck only a gramophone! If the gramophone hadn't been in the window nothing would have happened because Kathleen would have gone on and forgotten about the house. She just lifted the window and climbed in.

The gramophone had a big soundbox and speakers; I think it was His Master's Voice because when my father was alive we had one with a picture of a little dog on it and he holding his ear to the soundbox. We used to buy loads of records in Smithfield for we all loved music.

Kathleen went into the house and got out the records, Bill Haley and rock and roll and 'Walking my Baby Back Home'. She put on an old dance dress belonging to the woman of the house, a dress with veils on it, and she got down to the rock and roll. The spring on the gramophone would run out, the voice would go real long so she would wind it up again and back she'd go to the dancing. She opened the window and put the horn of the soundbox out through it the way the children could hear the music and even the horse looked over.

Then Willie with his two big bony knees and his short

DEREK SPEIRS (REPORT)

Father Michael Mernagh being forcibly removed by the gardai while trying to prevent the eviction of travellers in Firhouse

trousers and his real skinny legs got down to the rock and roll on top of the four-wheeler. But I was always the worrier, the wise one, and I was crying. I was afeared someone was going to come along and we'd all be taken. Whenever anyone asked us where were our mother and father we always said, 'Mother's gone to the shops and Father's after the horses,' the way they get loose and stray off. The small children didn't know what was going on and I was at Kathleen, 'Come on, come on, we'll all be sent to a home and we'll never get out.' But she stayed there for about three hours, dancing, dancing.

Then she took off the dress and put it back hanging in the wardrobe — the woman didn't know what was after going on in it! She pulled down the window and never stirred anything the way no-one would know she'd been there. We never took anything, it was the gramophone, the music, because we were always on our own and we used to be very lonely.

When Kathleen came out from all the dancing she was so tired that she fell asleep in the back of the cart and Willie had to do all the driving.

I was always worried about getting into trouble though we never stole money or goods just milk or a few eggs. In the country there'd always be two or three big churns at the end of the farmer's avenue and we'd come along with our cans and dip into the churn. We'd take a can of milk and we'd all get a drink from it, that was the kind of thing we did and that was how we survived.

We'd stay in a country town till we had it all hawked, till all the houses were done and the people were sick of us calling. Then we'd move on to a different place, going backwards and forwards to Portadown and Lurgan and all around but we wouldn't move too far from Armagh.

There was an old man in Portadown called Frankie Hamill; we called him old, but he wasn't really, he was old as we were children. He came from a settled family that always lived in Portadown, they used to deal in horses and various things. He loved the travellers and their way of life and the songs they used to sing, so no matter where they were camping around Portadown he'd find them.

When we were camping on a lonesome road about four miles outside Portadown Frankie used to come along every night to see us. We could hear him coming from about two miles off: the horse would be galloping and Frankie would be singing at the top of his voice 'With my Dog and Gun', it's a real old song, 'By a mountain stream a moorcock crows'. He had a real loud voice, even when he'd be speaking, you wouldn't have to listen because you could hear him a mile off.

We used to love to see Frankie coming for we had no friends and every night we'd be waiting for the sound of the horse galloping. Frankie would gather up a big bundle of sticks and he'd fill two buckets of water and he'd sit with us till about ten o'clock and we were glad of this for company. He'd sing and sing and we'd all join with him — he was a real happy person. When he'd be going home he'd say, 'Well, ye're God's own children, He'll look after ye.'

He'd get back on his horse then and ride into Portadown, it was like a cowboy movie with him riding into the sunset!

Old Frankie was really the only friend we had. The white horse used to go like the wind but we hadn't the sense to get shoes on it; a horse needs shoes every so often but we let it go without and it went lame, the front hooves just split up along with sandcracks. When that happens the hoof has to have clips on it so it'll grow back together and it has to have rubbers inside the horse-shoes. Frankie took our horse into Portadown and he got all this done and it was really great of him.

The horse got better, the lameness was off him and he was able to walk so we shifted out of Portadown one day, I think it was to Lurgan. When we went we missed old Frankie. We used to be happy in the daylight, we'd be around the fire, cooking and washing the children. Then we'd start telling funny stories all about Paddy Irishman and Paddy Englishman and Paddy Scotchman, and Paddy Irishman was always the villain.

When it got dark we'd feel a bit cowardly. Maybe the bushes would rattle with the wind and there'd be cows outside eating off the bushes and they'd be pulling the ditch and you'd hear it crackling. Then the little ones would gather in tight to me and they'd say 'Little Nan, is there any ghostses around?' and I'd say, 'No, there's no such thing as ghostses,' and then they'd hear the bushes moving and they'd catch on to me and they wouldn't let me go.

I remember one night when it was very, very cold and the

ground flooded. The water went in under the beds and the old blankets were soaking wet. My little brother, Peter, he was hardly two at the time, got very sick with his chest in the middle of the night. He got boiling hot. Here were we with no doctor or adult to help us.

Years ago when children got a high temperature they were wrapped up in blankets; everyone did this, even settled people, the children were put in the warmest thing and sweat would be coming out through them. Today if you bring them to hospital they're stripped, and cooled off with a fan on them. But we wrapped Peter in a blanket and said prayers for him. He was roasting hot for he had some kind of chest infection. He was very bad for days and we were boiling milk for him and keeping him in bed. He came all right and then he was sound as a bell, he was running around a few weeks after in his bare feet.

We never had a doctor; when the children got sick they just had to get out of it themselves. In the wintertime when they had to walk around in their bare feet they'd pick up thorns. We had to get them out with a needle and disinfectant or their feet would turn septic and they wouldn't be able to walk. Kathleen would hold up the children's feet and I would get out all the thorns with a sewing needle so I was the nurse or the doctor.

6.

A peculiar young fellow

Kathleen was always the strong one, she was only fifteen but she looked sixteen or seventeen and when she was with us we had a big person to lean on. She was always laughing and singing and she used to keep us sort of alive she was that happy.

One day, when we were camping in Portadown, Kathleen told us she was going away. She had this thing about England, a lot of Father's people were there, married to setted people. She said, 'Now my mother will be out in the morning, you'll be all right.'

It nearly broke my heart Kathleen going away because she was the favourite. We were so attached to each other we shared everything, my other sisters were just tiny. When she was going she said to me, 'Now some day I'll come back for you.' But I didn't see her for years and years until I was married and had a child.

She went off to get the bus or train back into Belfast and we watched her go. She walked along this real straight road with her bundle and we watched her until she was out of sight. We couldn't bear to lose her.

She went back into the Bog Meadows and Mrs McAloon and her husband looked after her and then she went to England. But she had no-one there to go to. She was only fifteen and she had no money, no education. When I grew up I was always thinking what kind of life she must have had.

So Kathleen was gone, the one that kept the life in the place. We'd remember when she'd go driving the horse and singing 'Whip crackaway! Whip crackaway!' and her lovely hair blowing in the wind.

I turned into a very sad person after losing Kathleen; it was as if everyone that I loved was going away and not coming back:

my father, my mother, my oldest sister that I was always with. I used to go outside the ditch and cry for hours; I didn't want to cry forenenst[7] the children to upset them.

Kathleen thought my mother was getting out of prison the next day because she'd done the nine months for stealing the scrap. But when she was due to come out the fine for camping came up against her and she had to do another three months.

Now it was the cold, cold winter. The children never had any shoes and they used to cry with the cold. Living in a tent was awful; sometimes when we'd put it up it would blow away. Willie used to get the water and the sticks and I'd go out and do the hawking. I used to have to walk miles and miles. If you were in Belfast where the houses were close together you could get the bus to them but in the country you'd have to walk so far to every farmer's house. Maybe the dog would attack you up a lane or the farmer would run you with a pitchfork. Some of them were very rich, like millionaires.

Where will you turn now, where will you bide
Now that's the work all done and the farmer does
not need you
And the council will not heed you and the terror
time has come.

The woods give no shelter, the trees they're bare
Snow falling all around
And the children they're a 'crying
And the bed on which they're lying
Is frozen to the ground.

The snow will not lift and the stove will not draw
There's ice in the water churn -
Trying to do a bit of washing
And the kindling will not burn.

The day I wouldn't get from begging or selling things we would go in and rob eggs or butter. In the North the farmers would have a dairy in the middle of the yard for the butter and eggs and milk. There would be water running through it and it would be real cold and spotless clean.

One day we tried loads of houses and no-one would give us

anything, they just ran us away from the place and set the dogs on us so I went into a dairy. The country butter was all made in circles with little shapes on it: there'd be a little cock of hay or a sheaf of oats printed into it. I filled up my basket with duck eggs and circles of butter and I filled up my can with milk. The butter was lovely, when you'd cut it you'd see the water running through it.

We came along the road and an old woman came out of a very poor cottage. She looked at all the children in the four-wheeler and she couldn't believe we were on our own. 'Och, the poor wee wains,' she said, 'where did ye come from?' She was about eighty but she was very sensible she wasn't like some old people. She brought us into the house and sat the children on stools and made the tea.

There was no-one there but the old woman and a few little chickens and bantams; I felt sorry for her. Willie had this thing for gathering mongrel dogs and kittens, all kinds of animals he'd bring back and he'd be feeding them whatever food would be in it and I often gave out to him for giving milk to the dogs. He asked the old woman for one of the bantams, a tiny little coloured hen.

The woman went out the back with Willie and when I saw her going I took the basket of eggs and butter and I put half of them in a cupboard. I filled up her jug with milk from the can I was after stealing from the farmer. Then we did little things for her around the place, gathered wood, swept the floor and washed the dishes before we went on. We never told the old woman about the things in the cupboard — I suppose she must have thought the fairies left them there!

Sometimes we'd gather scrap, brass and copper and bits of things and we might save it up for a week and then bring it into town and sell it. Then we'd buy swag to sell over again. We went up to a farmer's house looking for scrap one day and the farmer ran us with a pitchfork — he was like a giant. He was after Willie — 'Don't come back here no more, you dirty little gypsy!'

Willie said nothing. He came down along the lane and the farmer after him, just for going up to the house, we didn't do anything. Willie came to the end of the lane and went on along the road in his bare feet, he was a great runner. I was behind him but the farmer passed me out, he was after my brother. Willie knew the farmer couldn't catch him and when he got along the road he looked back at him and put his tongue out: 'Big ears, with your two big ears! Baldy head, you won't catch me!' And then he sat down in the road and cocked up his two legs at the farmer. He was wild as a goat but it was an innocent kind of wildness.

Another day we were driving along the road with the four-wheeler. There was a prize bull in a field with a ring out of its nose attached to a big chain. It was tied in the middle of the field to a thing stuck in the ground. Willie went out to the bull with an old green skirt, my skirt — I was going mad over it. He let on to be a Spanish bullfighter and went at the bull — '*Olé! Olé!*' The roars of the bull could be heard two miles away! Willie really upset this bull; he was going too close to it and if it could have got out I'm sure it would have killed him.

With the noise the bull was making, pawing the ground and bellowing, the farmer came along with a blackthorn stick and he jumped across the gate. I was shouting at Willie, 'Willie, Willie, you're done!' but Willie wasn't a bit afeared, he got out through a little hole in the ditch.

One day we couldn't get anything to eat. We came to a farm with henhouses going for miles, they had hundreds of red hens that lay the brown eggs. We would steal food where it wouldn't be missed so we put Willie into a henhouse and he came out with a chicken under his coat, covered with feathers and dung and everything.

We lit a fire. Now the hen was alive: if Willie had killed it before he brought it out it would have been all right but the children saw it alive. I said to Willie, 'Now, it's your turn to take the chicken up the road and kill it — don't do it forenenst the children.' But Willie wouldn't do it. So we took out a ha'penny and tossed it and he had to do it in the end. He went up the road outside of the ditch and he killed the chicken. When he came back with it the tears were running out of his eyes.

'The poor hen is dead and you made me kill it.'

I plucked the hen and cleaned it out and boiled it. Not one of the children would eat it! They were really hungry for they had nothing to eat all day but they were crying, 'Oh, look what you done to the poor chicken.' There were an awful lot of funny things and good parts in our life but Willie never forgot the chicken.

We went on into Lurgan, it was a great place for the travellers years ago. Lord Lurgan's castle was in the middle of the town with a wall around it and a green space. The travellers would pull in their wagons beside the wall and that's where we camped; but we didn't mix with the others, we were always sort of loners.

Willie had heard Father telling us the story of Master McGrath, the greyhound that went down in history. A little boy was drowning him in a river and one of Lord Lurgan's men saved him. They brought him up and he turned into a great dog — he used to be on the old pennies. Willie went up to a house for a drop of milk for the tea, we never used have any milk in the morning, the children used to drink it. He brought back a little mongrel pup and it was mangy. I said, 'We're not keeping that puppy,' we already had a dog, 'we can't keep it, Willie, its hair is falling out,' but Willie said, 'That little pup was going to be drowned in the river and the same thing happened to Master McGrath and look at the way he turned out!' He imagined that this little mongrel pup was going to turn out like Master McGrath.

Another day we went into Lurgan, hawking all around the houses, we brought the children with us in an old pram. When we were done hawking Willie was really tired. He had a ha'penny left in his pocket but he could get nothing for it: the way people look at travelling children we wouldn't be served in some shops. There was one shop in the town on the way home and Willie thought he'd get a sweet or something there but we left it too late and the woman would give him nothing for the ha'penny. He was a very peculiar kind of a young fellow. He took the ha'penny and he fired it in over the walls of Lord Lurgan's castle. And he said to me, 'Did you see that ha'penny?' I said, 'Yes,' and Willie said, 'That'll be there when I'm an old man and if you come back here when I'm old you'll find it.' But Willie didn't live to be an old man. He was killed in England when he was only twenty-four. When I heard about him dying I thought of the ha'penny that he threw in over Lord Lurgan's castle.

It was like a fairy story in a way, all the little things that happened, the way we survived and the way we lived but it was a true fairy story.

The night before my mother got out of prison we were camped in a very lonely back road in Portadown and a heavy storm blew the tent away. The covers were gone and the rain just poured down, the children were soaking wet and crying with the cold. We couldn't get a fire going; the sticks were all wet and if we tried to light a match it kept blowing out.

There was an idle house nearby that the farmer used for holding straw and hay so we went into it. We opened up the bales of straw and laid blankets on them and put the children lying down. Willie got sticks and we lit a big fire on the floor in the middle of the house — it's a good job the floor was stone. The fire was going all night and it's a wonder we didn't go up in flames with all the straw, I don't know what saved us.

It was still stormy next day and raining so we stayed in the house and fried sausages on the fire. I didn't know that was the day mother was getting out of jail.

Next morning I cooked the breakfast and washed the children and brushed their hair. Then I said to Willie, 'You keep an eye and I'll go in and hawk Portadown.'

It was a long walk into Portadown, about four miles. I used always bring my little sister with me in my arms because she was so tiny I was afeared of leaving her behind. When I got into the town with the child on one arm and the basket of swag on the other I was tired out. I was hawking up and down, selling things, when I saw my mother walking along the main street. I couldn't believe it, I thought I was seeing things because I didn't know she was getting out. We never saw her for the full year she was in prison.

Mother took the child from my arms and the basket and she brought us into a cafe and got me some tea and chips and a bottle for the child. She kept looking at me; I suppose the way we were, with all the hardship we must have looked terrible.

When we came back along the children were all outside the house. They saw my mother and the older ones knew her but they didn't run to her, the younger children never even looked at her. They ran to me. 'Little Nan, little Nan did you get any sweets?' I used to bring them back a few sweets or biscuits.

It took them a while to get used to my mother, none of them

went to her. For the year I had been the mother and now instead of catching on to my mother's skirts they'd hold on to mine. I had been the protector and looked after them and cooked and washed for them.

We went back into the Bog Meadows and every day I'd go out begging and selling little things to get the price of food. Some days my mother would go out but she was better off looking after the children. I used to go up Andersonstown and Willie would always be with me. We were great pals, I felt he was sort of a man and I was safe with him although he was only tiny. We knew all the buses for the various parts of Belfast; we'd get one to City Hall and another one to wherever we wanted to go.

Coming home in the evening when we'd been walking all day we'd be tired out, our feet would be paining us. The buses would be full at five in the evening and Willie would say, 'I'm going to get a seat, I'm not able to stand till we get to the Donegall Road' — that's where we got off for the Bog Meadows — 'and the people walking on my toes.'

There was a trick shop in Smithfield where Willie used to buy stink bombs and white mice. Before he got on the bus he'd rub some of the stink bomb on his clothes and he was like a skunk! When the people smelled him they'd get up from their seats, they'd all move up to the front of the bus and Willie would be left a seat and I'd be let sit down.

Another day if he couldn't get a seat he'd take a little white mouse out of his pocket and let it crawl up his shoulder and along his neck. You'd see the people charging up to the front of the bus — some used to get off the bus altogether! Those were the kind of things that kept us going, that kept our hearts up.

7.

No ring on my finger

It was a summer's evening when we pulled into the fair green in Dundalk. I was sixteen and we were on our way to see my granny, my mother's mother, she travelled around Trim and the north side of Dublin. There were some travellers in the fair green already, the Joyces, my mother knew them but I didn't. That was the first time I saw my husband John but we didn't speak to one another that time.

The Joyces pulled out after about a week and went back to Dublin, to Finglas, because that was the great place for them, they've been there for years. They originally came from Galway but that's going back a long way. When we met my granny we went on to Finglas and pulled up where the Joyces were. A few weeks later we shifted with them and camped beside the Dodder river. It was a lovely place with the river and big rich houses all around.

John and I didn't go out together, not the way some people go out for a long time. My brother was always fixing old bikes and punctures and John used to come over and help him and his parents used chat my mother.

One day John's brother came up and said, 'John wants to know will you marry him?' He was ashamed to ask me himself! I said No, I wasn't even thinking about getting married. Mother said I was too young, I was only sixteen. John was twenty. But the travelling girls got married very young that time, at fourteen or fifteen. When you passed eighteen you were old, you were on the shelf.

There were a lot of match-made weddings years ago but even then some of the girls and boys would choose their own. But the parents were very strict; if you were going to the pictures with a boy you always had your sisters and brothers with you, you were never allowed out on your own.

We decided we would get married and my mother and John's mother went to see the priest in Donnybrook chapel and the wedding was set for two weeks later — at eight o'clock in the morning! I don't think there was ever anyone got married at that hour.

It was a winter's morning when we got married. I was wearing a cotton dress and I was frozen walking the two and a half miles to the chapel. There were no adults with us, just our little brothers and sisters. A few days before the wedding one of my sisters bought a barm brack and she found the ring inside it. This was the little brass ring I had on me getting married; it must have looked awful — the priest kept staring at it. When he had us married he said to my husband, 'Now I hope you'll look after her well for she's very young.' I must have looked even younger than I was.

We walked back along and we were really happy, we were singing like children. Our little brothers and sisters were making a laugh of us. I still did the cooking that day but in the evening John and I went to the pictures, it was *Seven Brides for Seven Brothers!* Years ago when someone got married the travellers would joke and raise fun and that night we found our bed full of nettles and thorns off the thistles. The next day was Sunday and I got up early and walked along by the Dodder river to Mass. My husband went over to his parents' camp so I was gone one way and he was gone the other but we got on well because I was used to coping and managing with money.

After we were married we stayed in Dublin for a few months but I didn't like Dublin at that time. I was reared in Belfast and I loved the North, I think part of you stays where you're reared. I knew a lot of people there whereas in Dublin I knew nobody and my husband knew everybody. I got around him and we went back travelling to the North. John's father and mother and my mother and the children came with us, we were always attached to one another.

We camped in Newry along by the big canal; there were other travellers there and families with girls about my age, I knew them from growing up in the North. One day we went in to hawk Newry. Some of us were selling things our husbands made — saucepans or tea drawers. I used to make flowers from nylon or paper or elder sticks so I had some in a basket. We had all the stuff sold by about three o'clock and we sat down on the path to count our money. There was great sharing among the women that time; if one had got a big piece of bacon she'd cut it and give another woman half; and if some got enough food and money by two or three o'clock and another woman didn't they'd all go on hawking again till they'd get for her. If one woman went to hospital to have a child another woman would take over her family so she wouldn't be worried.

While we were counting our money on the path one of the girls was smoking and I didn't like that. When we were growing up we weren't allowed to smoke or be vulgar, we were always supposed to be graceful. I was giving out to her, 'Girls shouldn't be smoking along the street.' She swore at me.

All of a sudden I heard a voice behind me: 'I have come for you and I want to bring you to a better place: you weren't made for this world.'

I had the money in my lap but I jumped up and it all fell around; I got that much of a shock I didn't even pick up half of it. I looked behind me and there was a man over six foot tall and very handsome. I don't know whether he was from earth or where he came from. He was dressed all in black, with a black topcoat, a black suit, black shoes and even his shirt was funny, it was like something a priest would wear. The only thing he had that was white was a sort of scarf like the stole the priest wears at confession or at Mass only it was completely white and it was down to his knees inside the topcoat.

I got afeared of my life and I said, 'What do you want me for?' He passed no remarks on the other girls or little boys but whatever he saw in me he said, 'I want to take you to a different place. You needn't be afeared — I don't want to hurt you.' I started crying. I was so innocent, I was only sixteen. I said, 'Go away.' He said to me in a soft gentle voice, 'It doesn't matter where you go or what you do I'll get you in the end.'

We started running and he was after us. Then he suddenly stopped and he was walking easy. We ran like the wind through the streets of houses but whenever we looked back he was still there. We ran up one little back street and there was no way out. He was standing at a lamp-post. We flew back but he didn't make a grab for us or run he just kept going real easy.

We went into a sweet-shop and this is how we missed him; we never saw him since. If I am alone now, if my husband is gone off in the winter and I'm in bed or sitting on my own I keep thnking about what this man said.

After that we left Newry with our wagon and horses and we went round to all the places I camped as a child. My uncle and aunt were with us, she was a Romany gypsy and great sport. My husband used to buy scrap and sell it over again to make money. We went to the fairs at Ballyclare and Ballycastle and I used to tell fortunes.

One day a farmer of about fifty came in to me. He was a bachelor and he asked me, 'Will I ever get married?' I said, 'What kind of a girl would you like now if you were getting married?' and he said, 'Bedamn it, a lass like yourself would do me lovely!' and I started laughing at him. He was from some big farm in the North and I said to him, 'A lass like me wouldn't be much good to you because I'm very skinny and I'd be no use on the farm!' And he said, 'Bedamn it, I wouldn't want you for the farm, it'd be for myself I'd want you!'

Going to the fair every year the same men and women would come to have their fortunes read and they'd say to me, 'Everything you told me would happen did come true and now I've come back for you to tell me something else important.'

When I read fortunes I hold the top of the person's hand and it's something like a power I have for I have always been psychic. I can tell if something is going to happen, but I can do nothing about it. Say if I was sitting in the caravan and I saw someone out on the road I might think to myself 'Oh, something terrible is going to happen to him.' I'll forget about it immediately and I'll turn away and then I might look out and see he's been knocked down. Or I might be outside getting water and see two men who haven't met for a while shaking hands and they're in great humour chatting one another. Then I'll say to myself, 'Oh, God, they're going to have a fight.' I might go in and start cooking and then I'll hear them fighting. A lot of travellers, if they're going to get bad news, will know about it two or three days before. You get this funny feeling, it's like a depression but you can't get out of it and you're watching the road for someone coming with bad news.

I can tell sometimes what someone is thinking and I often saw people getting embarrassed when I'd be looking at them. Maybe they're thinking 'This is a very unusual person for a traveller,' and I get the vibrations off them.

When I'd be done reading the fortunes we'd go around the fair, we'd look at the amusements and listen to the music — all life was there. Sometimes we'd win things, like a teddy bear or a piece of china and we'd buy Yalla Man — that's yellow toffee that you break with a hammer.

Did you treat your Mary Anne
To dulse and Yalla Man
At the ould Lammas Fair
At Ballycastle O?

From Ballyclare we went to Cushendall and Ballymena and we travelled around for about a year before we came back into Belfast. I was just seventeen and I was expecting my first baby. When the women from the Falls Road would see me they'd say 'Och, look at the poor wee lass!' I looked so young and they didn't even know I was married for I had no ring on my finger. About a week after the wedding I had a row with John and I took off my wedding ring and fired it across the ditch. Years ago it was supposed to be bad luck to throw away your wedding ring or do anything with it. I was days looking for the ring in the ditch but I never could find it. My mother used to bring me down to the clinic and all the women would keep looking at me, I was ashamed of my life.

My first little girl was born in the City Hospital in Belfast. It was the winter-time. All the other mothers in the ward used to be talking about doing up the nursery, what wallpaper and carpet they'd have and what kind of cot and pram they'd buy. I was listening to all this and I knew what I had to go home to — a big mucky camp.

When I came out of hospital we went out to the country and my husband gathered scrap. Then we went to Scotland with my uncle and aunt. I was expecting my second little girl — there was just a year between them. It was the middle of winter and when we got off the boat in Glasgow it was dark. I had the little one in my arms, she was about nine or ten months old, and my husband had a bundle and the cases, we didn't bring a caravan.

We didn't know where to go looking for a room or a flat and we had hardly any money. We went in a taxi to Nicholson Street, it's all bulldozed now, I think, and we got a room. It was a slum; the water used to run down the walls onto the floor, even the toilet was in bits — when it was flushed the water came out. There were rats and mice in the kitchen; it was just awful.

Then my husband got a room in another street, it was a slummy place too but it was better than the room we were in, at least the water wasn't running down the walls. This place had flights of stairs with landings and each landing had about five rooms off it, with a poor family in each one. Some of them were Irish, not travellers, and some were poor Scotch people. The way they were living was disgraceful. There was no bath and you had to wait in a queue for the toilet, there was only one little cooker in the kitchen and you'd wait in line for one woman to boil her dinner before you'd have your turn.

We'd have been better off in a caravan, at least it'd be cleaner and we'd have some kind of privacy.

I used to sit at the open door, I couldn't bear to look at this place we were living in. We were always thinking about Ireland; although we were sort of outcasts still we called it home and we'd think about getting back although we had no home to go to.

My sister Kathleen had been in Glasgow for years, working in a hotel. She used to write back to my mother so we got in touch with her and she came to see us. I was so glad to see her! She'd turned into a lovely lady, you'd think she was from a big posh house the way she was dressed and the way she had her hair. She spoke real English because she'd been in England for years.

But the happy person Kathleen had been was there no more. When John went out we would sit in the little room in Glasgow and the first thing would get into our mouths was Belfast and the Bog Meadows and her eyes would fill up with tears. I suppose there were thousands of girls down through the years gone to England like Kathleen with no money, no education, no-one to go to. What kind of life must she have had? She'd

DEREK SPEIRS (REPORT)

When Fr Niall O'Brien was held prisoner in the Philippines, I took part in this unusual protest at the American embassy in Dublin against US support for the Marcos regime.

1567
5492
11279
9764

been in a convent and learned all kinds of things, reading and writing, and then she got a job in a hotel.

Kathleen came up every day to see us and then she stayed with us for a few weeks; only for she came I don't know how I would have survived, I would have ended up in an asylum or something.

There was a poor Scotch woman with about six little children in a tiny room near ours and she was expecting a child. When Kathleen came this woman had just had her child in the bed. Over there you didn't have a doctor they sent a nurse but she hand't come. The baby was about nine pounds in weight and the cord was around its neck, it was choking and turning blue. My sister knew a lot, because she does a lot of reading as I do myself so she took off her coat and washed her hands. Then she lifted the child and turned it round, she got the cord from around its neck and left it nice and level out on the bed. She bathed the woman in the bed with a piece of facecloth. The poor woman hadn't got a clean sheet, blanket or towel so my sister brought up some clean sheets and blankets from our place and changed the bed. She was like one of those saints that come to help. The nurse didn't come for about an hour — the mother and child could have been dead.

When it was time for my little one to be born my husband rang for an ambulance but they sent a young nurse instead. It was something like the other woman — because we were poor we didn't matter. With the first child I had no problems, I was in hospital with good doctors and nurses and I had everything but this time I was very sick. The little room was tiny, the glass was broken in the windows and the wind came beating in and I was sick all night and all day. My sister looked after me and I don't know what I would have done without her because the nurse sat reading a love story at the fire. Kathleen did far more for me than any nurse.

The next night my little girl was born and she had a hernia, her whole stomach used to come out when she cried. The hernia was the size of an egg and it'd get real hard and turn blue. I don't remember a doctor ever coming to examine me or the child and I was in bed for weeks, I was that sick. I was so weak that when I tried to get out of bed to do something I'd fall, I must have needed blood or iron.

The little one was a year old and she was able to crawl around and come over to me in bed but I forgot about the baby. It wasn't that I wanted to forget but I was so weak and tired and I was always trembling in bed and still I was roasting. It was like a fever, the sweat used to pump out through me. The nurse came for a few days but then she stopped coming and she musn't have told anyone how sick I was.

My sister Kathleen did all the looking after for about two months until I got back on my feet. If she hadn't been there the baby would have died for sure because I wasn't able to get up and make bottles or change it or bath it.

When I was better we came back to Dublin. Here was Kathleen being left behind again after all the great things she did for me. When we were gone she was so lonely she said, 'I won't stay in Glasgow after this.' She went to London and got a job in a hotel there. She could never go back to the road because she couldn't stick the hardship any more, she was used to luxury and being clean.

Kathleen is married now, to a settled man in England. He's an architect and they have a beautiful house because they can do wonders with a house. They have six children and they're all very well educated, some of them are going to college, so she made a good life for herself. I went over to see her about seven or eight years ago. Sometimes her husband would come home from work real tired and Kathleen would be after moving the furniture around. The way settled men are they have their favourite armchair and he'd be looking for it to sit down and he'd say to Kathleen, 'What are you moving the furniture for?' and she'd say 'Well, I've shifted today!' The traveller was still in her after all those years!

I still miss Kathleen and I think about when we were children; when Father was alive we were so happy.

The doctors in Glasgow had said they could do nothing about the baby's hernia until she was three or four years old. It was getting worse; when she cried it would turn blue, it was like a small balloon. When we were back in Dublin I took her to a clinic and as soon as the doctor examined her he put a rubber belt on her. He said that it was a very bad hernia and she should have had a belt on the whole time. He told me to take her down to Temple Street immediately for an operation. The operation was successful and after it she was sent out to a convalescent home in Dun Laoghaire. When she was born she was very tiny, very underweight, so she was better off in hospital for the while.

When it was time for the baby to come home I went to collect her; she looked so tiny — her eyes were the biggest part of her. Standing at the gate of the hospital waiting for a bus my mind just went. My memory was gone. It must have been the effects of the birth because I wasn't really well for a long time after. I was on my own and I could think of nothing. I didn't know what I was standing there for or where the child came from. I saw people passing by but I couldn't even ask for help.

There was a chemist shop beside the hospital so I went in and tried to explain to the woman; if she had been clever she could have helped me but I suppose she thought I was mental. I was crying because I didn't know what to do. I went in then to a little chapel opposite the bus stop and I lit some candles and started to pray. My memory came back there and then. I thanked God when everything came back into my mind — at least I knew the way home.

After that we travelled the whole of England and the North of Ireland and back to Dublin again. We were always going: it was like following an elusive dream of some kind, as if you were looking for something and you didn't know what it was. We came back to the Bog Meadows, it was always the favourite place, and the Whiterock, Holywood Road, Show Road all of those places. After a few years we travelled back up to Dublin, to Cherry Orchard. We had five children by then, all girls.

The way the travellers were living in Cherry Orchard was awful. There was nothing only a mucky field, it hadn't even got grass on it. This was facing the door of the Cherry Orchard hospital. The travellers had little huts built with old bits of wood — it was like something you'd see in foreign countries, the way the poor people have to live in shanty towns. The little huts were all next to one another and in each one there'd be half a dozen children and a mother and father. There was no water or toilets. When it rained you'd think the bulldozers had been digging.

The rats were in hundreds. I remember sitting up one night

watching them take the food out of the press. One of them had a piece of bread and they were fighting over it and you could hear them all squealing. The children were getting sick, with diarrhoea, vomiting, everything. I was really browned off with Cherry Orchard, I used to sit down and cry when I couldn't keep the children clean. All the travelling women were the same, I wasn't special. When it rained the mud would come in like a river and when you'd wash the children they'd fall into it. There was no way of keeping a dry blanket or a clean towel, no matter how hard you tried you couldn't keep them clean.

I had a fight with my husband and when we have a fight I always go and I bring the children. They're like a little clutch of chickens, wherever the hen goes the chickens go. We had a little Mini car and I put the five children in it and headed off for Belfast. Even though we had no home there I thought Belfast was my home.

It was nearly dark when I was driving into Belfast. There was a policeman doing traffic duty and he pulled me up. 'Have you got a match, love?' he said. 'Of course, yes,' I said, and I handed him a box of matches. He said 'Will you try and light your lights then — you've no lights on!' I was so upset I'd forgotten about it.

I drove to Duncrew Street; there were factories there and a road that no-one used and the travellers used to pull into it. It was winter and I was sorry for going away, for leaving Dublin at all. The children were all very small and there was nowhere for me to go. I don't know if there was even Battered Wives at that time. I was completely lost. When you're married to someone for years since you were so young the two of you are attached and you're used to being together; and then when you have problems, if one doesn't advise the other one will.

The Mini was too small to sleep in. I went into an old van with no windows or doors and I tried to make a bed for the children. They were up crying with the cold, they were freezing. The wind and the rain would come in one side and out the other.

There were other travellers down from us but I didn't go near them, I never liked asking anyone for anything. I always liked to be independent. We were there for two weeks and it was worse than Cherry Orchard. Then my husband came and we went back with him.

They came to shift the travellers from Cherry Orchard but we wouldn't go, the same as now. If you shift out of one place you'll be hunted again and it's not worth moving. The bulldozers came and the little huts were all knocked down: it was an awful sight, it was cruelty. This was their homes — the travellers were left standing out on the road, the children too, with nowhere to go and no shelter.

8.

Waiting for something better

From Cherry Orchard we went to a big field near Ballyfermot. There was a factory a few miles away for taking lead from old car batteries and the shells were dumped for miles around. It was the summer and the children used to play outside. My fifth little girl, Julie, was two and a half. Sometimes she'd let her soother fall and then she'd pick it up and put it back in her mouth. The whole ground was contaminated with the batteries but we didn't know that, we never thought about lead poisoning.

Julie got very sick; she was vomiting and eating nothing. I even got Lucozade to see could she keep something down but the very minute I gave it to her she'd throw it up again because her whole inside was completely ruined. I took her to the doctor in a clinic at Ballyfermot and explained to him about her always vomiting. She was so sick, she never used to cry she was that far gone, and her teeth were black but it wasn't from dirt. The doctor never examined her, he just wrote out a prescription. It was for a bottle and I kept spooning it into Julie but it was like giving her water because it wasn't for lead poisoning at all.

One morning when I was holding Julie, trying to give her a drop of Lucozade, she went unconscious in my arms. It was as if she was dead because her eyes were wide open and she was so still. My husband had gone out, there was no-one there but myself and the other children. I was about eight months expecting but I ran into Ballyfermot with Julie in my arms. The phones were all broken and Julie was very heavy because she was a strong healthy child but I kept on until I met a lovely little settled girl who got me into a place to phone.

Julie must have been an hour unconscious before the ambulance came. She was taken into Our Lady's Hospital in

Crumlin and at first they didn't know what was wrong with her. After three or four days someone came out to the camp to look into what happened to the child. So I said, 'There's old shells of car batteries thrown away and there's nothing else she could have got poisoned from.' They took away a piece of car battery and they tested it and Julie's blood and they found she had lead poisoning.

My other four little girls were poisoned too so the five of them were in hospital together; Julie was very sick and so was Ann but the other three weren't so bad. I could go and see them any hour of the day or night and the sister in charge was a lovely woman. It's great to meet someone who'll understand you, not pity you because I hate pity.

Every night I used to go up to see Julie. She was unconscious for a long time, nearly two weeks. Sometimes I'd be very late but whatever time I went there was always a black doctor with her. It was strange because I always had a favourite saint and he was black — Saint Martin de Porres. I got a relic of him and I used to go round all the chapels praying all day, for Julie was dying, she was given up. She was in a little place on her own but I never saw the black doctor's face when he was sitting beside her cot. He'd have his back to the door and I had this nervous feeling that I couldn't go in, I couldn't go near Julie because I was afeared that she would die while I was standing there.

I had myself nearly worn out with crying and I was eating nothing so one day I went to talk to a priest. I wanted someone to speak to because I had no-one to lean on, and I was in an awful state. The priest was doing the lovely roses in the garden. I told him about Julie and he said to me, 'Do you see those roses? Aren't they beautiful?' and I said, 'They're lovely, Father', I always loved flowers. He said, 'They won't be there in the end of the summer.' I didn't know what he meant by it, he didn't give me any explanation. I went in then to the chapel and lit a candle and I kept thinking about what the priest said. I couldn't make out what he really meant.

That summer a film called *Sinful Davey* was being made in Ireland and they were looking for travelling women with long hair to be in it. I went along and got a part and it took my mind off the little one because I was broken-hearted over Julie.

A bus used to come along and collect us every morning, about seven o'clock, a great Big American tourist bus — to get a jaunt in it alone was just great. It took us out to Ardmore Studios in Wicklow. It was a lovely place; we'd be out there all day and we'd get our dinner and supper before going home.

The film was all supposed to be happening hundreds of years ago. I was trying to cover myself because I was expecting the baby but with the long old clothes I'd hardly be noticed. A pal of mine, Josie Connors, had a part with me. She was a beautiful travelling woman with long red hair and we were supposed to be two tarts in the film — the way we were dressed we looked just like tarts! I had an antique dress with a real low top; they painted my chest a pink colour and I said, 'I'm not going to wear that thing there — when I go to see the film I'll be made a show of!' They had to give me an old-fashioned scarf to cover it up. None of the travelling women would wear a dress with a low top. The dress I was wearing was sprayed and it fell to bits — you'd think I had it on for forty years.

I had a wine bottle full of red water and I had to let on to be drunk, they showed me the way to walk around. The bottle was made of candle grease and if I hit anyone with it it would go in pieces.

The film was about a prison with men locked up for years without seeing a woman. The women prisoners were in the top part of the prison; there was straw in the corner and two of the old travelling women really thought they were in jail! They were handed in a dish of meat, it was all painted red and the old women went mad — they thought they had to eat it. The men put a hole through the floor to get up to the women. A little small man was the first to come through and a travelling woman of about fifty grabbed him and put him in her shawl and ran away with him!

The film was a really great experience and it sort of took my mind off the little one in hospital. One day I went in to see her and she was coming through. The doctors and nurses were great and I think all the praying I did helped because faith is a wonderful thing. If you have a strong faith in God you can get through anything, you can always pick yourself up and start all over again because the strength of God is there to help you.

When Julie came round she was like a child a week old. She

just kept staring at the ceiling and she didn't know any of us. Ann had been very sick too and the doctor explained that the lead poisoning would leave some effect on her and it did. She has always been very bad with her nerves. It affected all the children in various ways.

Julie got better but when she came home from hospital she started taking epileptic fits. Sometimes she would have three or four fits in a day. I used to start screaming, I couldn't cope with it because it was something I could do nothing about. She should have been on tablets but if I brought her back to hospital she'd be held in for a couple of days and then she'd be sent home again. It was only after we went to England that she was put on Phenobarb but there's nothing much can be done for people with epilepsy. After seeing her with it for years I sort of got used to it and now if she gets a fit I know what to do: I put her lying on her side and she gets out of it.

After the baby was born, that was Tommy, our first son, we shifted into one of those old chalets in Labré Park, in Ballyfermot. They're awful places, they're like prison camps, they've got one tiny room for cooking, washing, sleeping and everything and only one little window with the sort of glass you couldn't see in or you couldn't see out of. I thought it was terrible to put travellers into places like this, they would have been better off to be let travel or to have proper houses with a bit of room.

We stayed in the huts for about a year but they really weren't fit to live in and my nerves got at me. I was closed in, in this room, and then I could do nothing for Julie.

Things were going very bad for us; it seemed everywhere we moved we'd be waiting for something better but something worse always happened. So we packed up whatever we had and went to England. We got in with some Irish travellers who had been there for years and my married sister and her family. We travelled around with them all over England for about two years. My husband used to tarmac and I used to go out the odd time selling things out of baskets. I couldn't go out every day because of the children and Julie taking the epileptic fits.

It was really awful in England because the travellers were being hunted and hunted. There were very few sites and only the children on them got any education, the ones who were moving got nothing. When you moved into one area two policemen on motorbikes would come and they would escort you out of their area and then two more would come from the other area and so you'd be moved on. You'd be shifted at six o'clock in the morning and get no food until eight or nine at night because you'd be looking for a place to pull in but if you found one the police would say, 'Move on, move on,' and you didn't know where to go. There was no way of getting education for the children or Confirmation or Communion.

Once you could pull in with your caravan
To a sheltered spinney or to open ground
But the law moved in with the barbed-wire fence
And they said that your camp was a prime offence
And told you to shift and keep on going
And move along, get along, move along, get along,
Go: move: shift.

We moved into Glasgow into the middle of the old slums. The people weren't used to travellers in this area and the children all came down and fired stones at the caravans and broke the windows. It wasn't their fault, they were really poor children and they didn't realise what they were doing.

My second little boy, John, was born in Bell's Hill in Scotland. There were a lot of Irish nurses in the hospital and they were very good to me. The doctor said to me, 'You're only twenty-seven, you should have something done with yourself. Look how many children you're going to have by the time you're forty.' Of course with my religion I would never do this. I said to the doctor, 'I know you mean well but I don't believe in having an operation not to have children.'

John was a week old when we came back to Belfast. He was born in Bell's Hill and he was christened in Belfast so he says to me now, 'Where am I from?'

We camped along the Show Road for about a year and we were left, we weren't shifted. Then we moved to Ardoyne; the travellers were all piled in together into one tiny place in the Bone. Some of them were born and reared there but nothing was ever done for them and the way they were living was really inhuman.

We shifted from one side of the Bone to the other and camped on a little hill with the red-brick houses all around. The settled people there were very good to us, they were just poor people who weren't getting their rights no more than we were. Their houses were tiny and they had nothing in them. When we went over with our churns they would never refuse us our water. We used to go in and chat with the women — this is how you find about people, by going in and speaking to them.

The troubles started. There were soldiers and jeeps everywhere, petrol bombs being thrown and tear gas. You'd see gangs of boys in the night-time and men firing petrol bombs and some of the soldiers being shot. Then the soldiers would fire back. When I grew up in Belfast I never thought I would see anything like this. It was really awful; it was like something you'd see on one of the movies but you'd never believe it could happen in real life.

I remember one night there was a riot going on right beside us and all the tear gas got into the trailer. You can't breathe with this gas, it goes up your nose and down your mouth and even into your ears — you feel as if you're smothering. Then if you try to draw your breath you get this stinging inside you. We had to move the children outside in the middle of the night and we got no sleep because the people were rioting all night and the soldiers were firing rubber bullets.

When Protestants and Catholics couldn't get on and they were afeared of living side by side they'd move from one area to another. They'd come along to the travellers and say, 'Can I have a lend of your lorry?' The travelling men would go down and move their furniture and whatever they had; they would spend their evenings helping people to shift.

At first in the troubles we were very nervous but then we got used to it, we just walked out on the street where people were rioting and we did our shopping and we weren't afeared. You might stand and look at what's going on and you'd just say 'Ah' and walk on. It's like seeing a cowboy picture.

9.

Go! Move! Shift!

Born in the middle of the afternoon
In a horse-drawn trailer on the old A5
The big twelve-wheeler shook my bed
'You can't stop here', the policeman said
'You'd better get born in some place else,
So move along, get along, move along, get along,
Go: move: shift.'

Born in the tattie lifting-time
In an old bow tent near a tattie field
The farmer said 'The work's all done,
It's time that you was moving on
You'd better get born in some place else,
So move along, get along, move along, get along,
Go: move: shift.'

Born on a common near a building site
Where the ground was rutted with the trailer's wheels
The local people said to me
'You'll lower the price of property,
You'd better get born in some place else,
So move along, get along, move along, get along,
Go: move: shift.'

Wagon, tent or trailer-born
Last week, last year, or in far-off days
Born here or afar, seven miles away
There's always men nearby who'll say
'You'd better get born in some place else,
So move along, get along, move along, get along,
Go: move: shift.'

DEREK SPEIRS (REPORT)

A Minceir Misli march through central Dublin in the summer of 1985

Ulster
Bank
Irish
DRUMM

After about two years in Belfast we came on down to Dublin to Coolock. It used to be a favourite place with the Joyces, they camped there for hundreds of years, in the old village by the chapel. My husband's people were always there so he headed straight for them when we came back. But we weren't left anywhere, we were shifted from place to place and the children got hardly any schooling. My older children only went for a couple of months to get their Communion and Confirmation because the sacraments are very important to the travellers. I got Julie going to school three times but she used to take fits and then when she was out of them she would be so embarrassed. Other children called her names so she threw up school altogether and wouldn't go any more.

My third little boy, Patrick, was born in St James's and he was christened when we moved over to Finglas. We stayed there for about two years until Elizabeth was born but the Corporation kept shifting us, from one field to another. People say to us, 'Will you not settle down?' but we don't get the chance because we're hunted from place to place.

The winter sky was hung with stars
And one shone brighter than the rest
The Wise Men came so stern and strict
And brought the order to evict
'You'd better get born in some place else
So move along, get along, move along, get along,
Go: move: shift.'

The day before Elizabeth was born we pulled into a little green space in Finglas; it was the middle of winter and it was freezing cold. I was in labour all the next day but the Corporation sent men along to shift us and the bulldozers pulled us out. We had to shift whether we liked it or not. We moved down beside Cardiff Bridge, there are new houses built in that space now. Everything was upside-down: when you move a caravan you can't have a fire in it so the little ones were freezing. I had to go on into hospital to have the baby but all I was worried about was leaving the rest of the children. I went to St James's again and the sisters and nurses were really great — they've always been good to the travellers up there.

When I came out of hospital Elizabeth was christened and we moved over to Rathfarnham. We kept getting moved and after about a year we came back to Finglas and camped along by the side of the road near the football grounds. Then the guards started harassing us.

If you're a traveller you're not supposed to have nice things but I've always loved beautiful things. Years ago down along the quays in Dublin you could go into the antique shops with a few shillings and you'd pick something up. Maybe it'd be all dirty and dusty but you'd bring it home and wash it and it'd be really lovely. I love old things — a little piece of old china is part of the past. I have china from every place we travelled in England and Scotland and the North and I have a silver kettle on a stand and a silver punchbowl; I got them for a few pounds before I had any children.

One night the men went off to have a pint and I was alone with the children. The guards came over from Ballyfermot and started searching the place. We had some money saved up to buy a mobile caravan and when they looked in the drawer they saw it. 'Where did you get that?' they said. 'It's our own money,' I said, 'we're saving up to buy a mobile caravan.' The guards took all the money out of the drawer and they took my silver kettle and the dish and they brought me off to the barracks, to a little back room in Finglas police station. When John came back about eleven o'clock I was missing but when he came up to the barracks, the guard[8] in the office didn't know we were in the back room. He said 'There's no-one here, there's no Nan Joyce here.' I was nearly getting into a bad row over it because some men get very nasty if you're not there at night-time.

The guards counted the money — you know the way you throw money into a drawer without counting it, I didn't know exactly how much there was. They gave me back the money in the end but they took my silver things over to Ballyfermot police station and threw them all into a cardboard box. A few days later they put them on the television, on *Garda Patrol*, asking the owner to come along and claim them. I went over to Ballyfermot police station but they wouldn't believe me. One of the guards, a detective, was real cheeky and he kept shoving me out and saying, 'Where would you get them things? They're not yours.' So we had no chance of getting our things back because they didn't believe the travellers should have anything. In the end a settled man we knew went over and told the guards that he knew John for so long and that we had the things in the trailer for years and years. So they gave them back to us. But we'd never have got them back by ourselves.

About nine years ago, just before Richard was born, we were staying over in Ballymun and every second morning the guards were in at us before I was up out of bed. I don't know what they were looking for or what they were up to because my husband wouldn't steal a match and I would never steal anything now. When I was a child I often stole food, I admit it, but that time you had to steal to survive but since I got married I've never stolen anything. But the guards don't believe this and when they didn't find anything they never apologised.

Sometimes when I'd be in bed in the morning I'd waken up and see them all in the caravan. I'd say to them, 'Could you wait outside till I get my clothes on please?' I'd try to keep myself covered with all these strange men in the trailer but they'd come out with these funny remarks, 'Oh, don't mind us, we've wives of our own.' Just because they say they're married they think they have the right to see women getting dressed in the morning. Sometimes they would show a warrant and more times they wouldn't; they were detectives, they weren't in uniform so I couldn't even take their number.

I got really tormented with them. They'd turn out every drawer and every press, they even took all the food out of the cupboards. They'd take the children out of bed in the night and turn the mattresses over. We'd been there a long time and we wanted to stay because the children were going to school but I got so fed up I told John to move. It was the guards made us move not the Corporation, if it wasn't one person it was another.

I grew up with a fear of the guards but now that I'm a middle-aged woman I'm not against them and I really believe in law and order. The way we live we've no phone or address and if we need an ambulance or a doctor in a hurry, the first place we'll go is the garda barracks and they will do it all and be very good at it. Guards can be nice people and understanding and still not neglect their duty. But in Dublin for the last ten years it's been awful, some of them are going round like Hitler's men. I don't think the Minister for Justice knows about it because you have to be with people the whole time to know what they're up to. When you have a flock of dogs one dog will be like a saint when you're looking at him but when he's out of the noose he's eating sheep.

Soon after Richard was born an American woman was doing a book on the travellers and getting publicity for it on the *Late Late Show*.[9] She asked my aunt, Nan Donoghue, to go on the show with her and my aunt asked me along for company. When my aunt saw all the lights and cameras where Gay Byrne was, she got cold feet and shoved me on instead — I'd only come along to watch. Gay Byrne started speaking about the book so I said I wasn't there about the book — I had come to speak about the conditions the travellers were living under. Ever since I was very young I've been speaking up, I was always the one to give back cheek, I wasn't afeared of what would happen but it's only since I went on television and got things in newspapers that I got my voice heard.

The day after the *Late Late Show* there were people from the newspapers banging at the caravan door all hours and a couple of days after that, *Woman's Way* magazine did a big article about me. I was sort of cover girl on the front of it with the child in my arms. That was Richard, our youngest boy. Elaine was born about two years later, she's our last child.

One night Richard had us up crying with his teeth, some of them had tiny pinholes where they were going bad. We took him to a hospital on the north side because we thought it would have more facilities than a dentist, I thought he could have the teeth filled or something.

On the way into the hospital we met an old man who was in charge of parking the cars. We told him about Richard and he said, 'Ah, sure, leave his teeth till they all fall out when he's seven and he'll get new ones — it's very cruel bringing him to a dentist at that age!'

When it came to my turn I brought Richard into a sort of ward. There was a glass partition on the left-hand side; the door was open and we could see people lying in bed unconscious with blood running out of their mouths. It was like something from a horror movie, Richard got into a panic straight away.

The dentist was a big strong man with hairy arms. He had his sleeves rolled up and he was wearing a green apron like a butcher's — it was all stained with blood. He didn't talk to me or tell me what he was doing, it was as if I wasn't there and he didn't explain anything to Richard. A three and a half year old is quite sensible but he didn't even speak to him, or coax him up the way you'd do with any child. He just put chloroform on a piece of cotton wool, it must have gone back a hundred years, and held it up to the child's face. Richard was very strong and he wouldn't pass out, he kept kicking and working his arms and twisting his head and he never stopped screaming. He must have thought he was going to be murdered. The nurse took Richard out of my arms and told me to wait outside.

When I went back in he was sitting on one of the beds beside all the people who were unconscious and he was screaming, 'I want to go home, I want to go home!' He caught onto my hair and wouldn't let it go until we were out of the hospital. He was in shock; he kept trembling and screaming and I couldn't get him out of it, I slapped his hands and everything. Blood was running out of his mouth — they had pulled out his teeth.

Richard never was the same happy child again. He got in the way that when he saw a man coming to chat my husband he'd come screaming into the trailer and he'd catch hold of my skirt and he wouldn't let it go. He was having nightmares every night so I took him down to Temple Street. I tried to explain but some doctors won't listen; they should listen to parents who brought the child into the world and looked after him since the day he was born. This doctor seemed to get the idea that we were being cruel to Richard at home — but he was always a sort of a pet and he still is.

Richard is nine now and he's still nervous. A little boy that age will sort of stray off and you'll be always calling him but Richard never stirs from the place, he won't even go up to the shop if he wants sweets.

We moved over to the Kilmore Road and camped beside a little graveyard from Artane School. There was just our family and my daughter and son-in-law because we were always loners, we didn't like to be with crowds of other travellers. The children were at school every day so they didn't get into trouble and they were in bed early in the night.

The Statdust[10] opened just across the road from us. My daughter and son-in-law loved music and we all went in the the first night and had a great time. They had none of this thing of not serving travellers or blacks or anything like that.

The man who owned the place where we were camped wanted us out because he was building a shopping centre but we wouldn't move. If you kept moving you'd be going until the day you die, and if you went every day they'd shift you every day. A court order was taken out against my husband and son-in-law. My husband is different to me, he'll do what he's told but I won't. I said to him, 'Doesn't matter about the court, we still won't shift.' Sometimes you get tired doing what you're told, you can do it for the right and you can do it for the wrong. But then two squad cars full of guards arrived—just for two men, you'd think they were after committing murder, and they were brought to court for camping. So we had to go.

Once you could settle for a week or two
On a public common or a riverside
But the council chased us off the sites
And they said 'You people have no rights
You'd better get moving some place else
So move along, get along, move along, get along
Go: move: shift.'

We shifted down to Coolock, near Priorswood. We were there a few months and we got the children back into school again. It was the same school but they missed a few days on account of us being shifted and not knowing where to go. It's awful on the children because you're taking them out of school and putting them back in again and then they don't want to go at all because they can't settle down. They're afeared the caravans will be gone when they come back, especially a nervous child like Richard. When it was time for him to go to school he wouldn't go in, he got into a panic. There was a lovely teacher in the site at Coolock. Before she'd take the children in at all she'd come out and chat to them and get to know them for a few weeks. I explained to her about Richard and she came out every day at dinner-time and she got around him, 'Now, Richard, it'll be lovely at school,' and she'd bring him in and show him round for a minute and then let him home again. That's the way we got him going to school but only for she was so understanding and so kind he never would have gone.

10.

The will of God?

Our first grandchild, Mary's little daughter Anna-Marie, was born when we were in Priorswood. We always tried to keep the place tidy where we were camping, especially with young children around. We'd burn the dirt and use Jeyes fluid around the caravans. But then the binmen went on strike and people started dumping their rubbish on us. There were plastic bags in hundreds coming from cars and lorries and vans, just dumped at our place. I suppose people said 'They're travellers, they're ignorant, they're in the dirt and they won't mind more.'

The little boys were rooting all these bags to see what was inside them and they were bringing in bottles of tablets and old half bottles of medicine, they could have been posioned.

One night I was sitting up late, doing a bit of sewing. It was nearly eleven o'clock and the children were all in bed for hours when a big container lorry came in and I wondered where it was going in the middle of the night. It drove over along the ditch behind us and dumped a whole container of dirty stuff from a hospital — syringes, and dirty bandages and rubbish. My husband went over to see what they were doing and he said to me, 'I have to set fire to this load over here — if it's there in the morning the children are all going to get sick or they'll be poisoned.'

There were loads of rats around the caravans from the rubbish. The milkman was coming and sometimes when I'd go out to get the milk the tops would be gone off the bottles. I thought the birds had picked them off but one morning I went out real early and there was a rat drinking the cream from the top of the milk. Years ago in Belfast I knew children who got meningitis from rats.

Anna-Marie was just starting to walk and she was real cute.

Children learning to walk are so proud of themselves but they don't know what's wrong — they keep falling! My daughters love disco music and I remember one evening they had the radio on and the child kept shaking herself and trying to dance. She was heavy and strong because she was very well looked after. Mary thought the world about her, she wouldn't buy herself even a pair of shoes — all the money would go on swanky things for the child.

Next morning Anna-Marie was very sick. After having a big family you know an awful lot. If ever any of the grandchildren are sick they're brought in to me. If I say, 'Well, she doesn't need to go to hospital, she just has a cold,' that's all right, or if I say, 'Oh, she's very sick, take her down to the hospital' she's brought down. So when the child was brought in to me I knew she was dangerously ill, you wouldn't need to be a doctor to see that. She was crying and crying and her eyes were very peculiar — they were kind of foggy and tired. One minute she was freezing cold and then she was hot and then she'd go back cold again. Her neck seemed to be very stiff.

I said to my daughter and son-in-law, 'Take her down to the hospital,' so they brought her down to Temple Street. I don't know the name of the doctor who treated her that morning; she was put under a fan for a couple of hours and then she was sent home. She should have been admitted; it'd be different if she just had a cold but if you had any brains at all you'd know that she was dangerously ill, from the way she was crying and her eyes and her neck was so stiff-looking.

When they came home from the hospital my daughter brought the child in to me. She was screaming and screaming — she was in terrible pain. I said, 'Put her to bed and maybe you could give her a couple of baby aspirins or something that might cool her down.' But she was in so much pain from her head that she couldn't stop crying. Every hour I would run over to my daughter's caravan to see how she was getting on. Any other time when I would go in the child would put up her little hands for me to lift her, because she'd know that I would take her out in the fresh air for a walk when her mother wouldn't have the time to do it. But that day whenever I put my hands near she'd let out this unmerciful scream.

We were wondering would we bring her back to hospital but

what could we do after she'd been to one of the leading hospitals? You'd say, 'Well, the doctors must know more than we know and there must be nothing wrong with her.' The same as I'm a mother and if I'm cooking eggs in a pan I know they're eggs I'm frying. But when you bring a child to a doctor you're leaving that child's life in the doctor's hands.

We stayed up with Anna-Marie until one o'clock in the night-time and then I said to Mary, 'I'll go over and get a little rest,' because I was tired. 'Come over and see me if she gets any worse.' The child was still screaming, she'd been screaming from that morning. After twenty minutes Mary came over and she was roaring and crying. She said, 'The child is all broken out in black spots.' 'Oh,' I said, 'it must be the measles,' because they get a bit spotty and funny with the measles. I ran over with Mary and I got the shock of my life when I looked at Anna-Marie. I couldn't believe it. When I was a child I saw two little children dying with convulsions in a tent — they turned blue all over. But this child was all out in black spots. Some of them were as big as five pence and others the size of tenpences and they were all around her forehead and the back of her ears, on her face and body. She was barely able to breathe; she was moaning and still she was screaming, the pain must have been terrible. I told my other daughters that the child was dying, that she wouldn't live till morning but I didn't tell Mary because she was so upset.

We brought the child back down to Temple Street and three doctors got around her and they did their best to save her. They really cared. There was one young lady doctor and she was a great person, she fought all night to keep the child alive, she fought so hard. But if only she had been there that morning . . . the other doctor sent the child home and she dying of meningitis.

When the child died at six o'clock in the morning the young doctor sat down and cried with my daughter. She put her arms around her and they cried together.

Mary was in an awful state after her child died. She got very bad with her nerves. She'd just sit in her caravan crying and crying and no matter when you'd go in she'd have the child's doll in her arms. My heart was broken looking at her. And for the little one: I was just like her mother, I was so attached to her.

If they'd admitted the child that morning and they couldn't save her you'd say, 'Well they did their best.' But the doctor sent her home though her neck was stiff and her eyes were foggy. I said, 'I'm not letting that doctor away with it, because too many people got away with too many things in my lifetime.' I don't blame all the doctors in Temple Street because they are very good, some of them, and the nurses are absolutely great, I don't want them all to get the blame over one that did wrong but I was really tormented looking at Mary.

A settled woman told me about free legal aid and I went to a solicitor in the Northside Shopping Centre. I asked her had I case and she told me to go down and collect some papers from the hospital. I think it was the admission sheet. They would have filled in a form for the child and the name of the doctor would have been on it and what they treated her for because he didn't treat her for meningitis.

I went back down to the hospital to get the doctor's name.

When I asked the hospital nun about the doctor, what did she say to me? 'It's all the will of God'! I couldn't believe it — for a nun to say that. We blame God for all the bad things that happen but we don't thank him for the good things. If you go out on the road and kill someone and you're drunk people say, 'It's the will of God.' It's not the will of God. The God I know and pray to doesn't do this to children. I said, 'Sister, how could you say the like of that and you a nun? God doesn't do that to anyone, God doesn't do those things.' She told me the doctor was a great doctor but she never gave me his name. I said, 'Sister, how could he be a good doctor when he sent a child home that was dying.'

I could get no satisfaction. I went back to the solicitor and she told me to get some papers fom the hospital. The same nun sent me to another place down the town and when I got there what did they give me only a death certificate. I took it to the solicitor and she photocopied it but this wasn't what I wanted at all.

After a few weeks the solicitor said I had a case. Then my daughter had a nervous breakdown and she had to go to the nerve hospital in Portrane so I just dropped the whole thing. It really hurt me to drop it, looking at Mary and thinking of the little one.

One summer's evening I was out at the hospital waiting to see Mary. The waiting room was all glass. Outside was a big avenue with trees on one side and a lawn with daisies on the other, and I could see the old asylum, a red-brick building with copper spires. I felt very tired and tormented. All the poor women came down the avenue with the nurses, big strong women. Some of the patients were screaming and more of them were crying. Life can turn you if you haven't got strong will-power. I know it's not right to feel sorry for people because I hate pity myself, but I started crying because it broke my heart looking at them: some of them were only young girls.

I always carry a little diary in my pocket and if I'm waiting somewhere I put something down. I had just started writing a little poem about looking at those women when strong sun came in my eyes and I couldn't see a ha'porth. Someone who didn't believe in God would never believe me but I got a funny feeling that God was very close, that he was closer to the asylum than he was to any other place. A lovely sort of eerie feeling came just for a minute and then it disappeared. I had been really heartbroken looking at the women but now I didn't feel as sorry for them. When they came into the waiting room I was able to sit down and laugh and chat with them. They all gathered round me — I'm that kind of person — I sat in the middle of the whole lot of them. One of the girls had tried to commit suicide but there was nothing really wrong with her; Mary's nerves were a bit at her but she wasn't bad altogether. I've always had this will-power that I can get up and fight on again, but we're not all as strong as each other and people who give up can't help it.

The Corporation decided to shift us from Priorswood. There were a good few travellers along the road and none of us would leave. The little children were going to school and we were browned off moving. One morning, before some of the children had had their breakfast, the Corporation lorries arrived. There were vans of guards with them — I never saw so many guards in all my life in the one place — just to shift a few helpless travellers.

I don't think the guards should be involved with evictions because it turns the travellers against them. If the county council or corporation can't get you out then the guards come up and then the teenagers and the children think everybody is against them and there's no-one on the traveller's side.

Some of the travellers wouldn't leave and their caravans were towed away. I protested and said, 'No, we're not shifting,' because you can't keep running. I went up to phone the papers — people have to see the way they're carrying on. A woman from the *Times* or the *Press* came and she reported some of what happened.

We had bought a lovely mobile caravan for the teenage girls, it was nearly new and there was a room in it and a little dressing table. We had saved up a long time to buy it because girls do need their own place, they need their privacy. The Corporation bested us and took it away. What can you do against big loads of people?

I went on in the caravan with the children the way I'd know where it was and I could come back then and tell my husband. But the lorry wasn't made for towing, it was too high, and the caravan fell in bits. In the middle of Ballymun, right at the roundabout, it broke in pieces. The little children from the flats came out and gathered round it; the wheels fell off and the sides broke because of the way it was shaken when it was towed. They dragged it on to Blanchardstown and left it on the side of the road, it couldn't be moved any more. I was really tormented: if they'd even left it in a field it'd be better but they left it right on the road in the middle of a heap of mud and muck right up to the door. The children were all crying they were that upset.

I got a lift with my brother back to Priorswood and I was really tormented with what they were after doing. I jumped on top of one of the men from the Corporation and pulled his cap off, and I scratched him and called him 'Bogman' — all over the caravan. Some of the guards started laughing at me.

They were coming with the same lorry to take our trailer and break it up and leave it on another road. We had an old car but we had no towbar on it because we weren't thinking of shifting. My husband said to them, 'If you wait for a while I'll get the loan of a car to tow it away because you're going to break it in pieces.' But they wouldn't listen and they had the trailer attached to the lorry and the back was dragging on the ground. This was our home and it was all we had!

My husband got up on the back of the lorry to stop them. All he was doing was asking them to leave the trailer and he'd get the lend of a van or lorry and he'd tow it himself. But the guards got up and pulled him down by the hair of his head and dragged him along the ground. Then they lifted the trailer off the lorry and my husband got the loan of a car with a towbar. But he'd had that bad of a going-over that he wasn't able to drive. So I had to do it.

We didn't know where to go because some of the children were in the broken caravan in Blanchardstown and some of the children were with us. We went on up across the road from Darndale — there are white swanky-looking houses there, with a big high wall round them. I said, 'We'll pull in here' — it was about half a mile from where we'd been camping'and we'll go and collect the other children.' All we wanted was to pull in for a few hours to get a drop of tea; we had no tea that morning. The very minute we pulled in a gang of people came out from the houses. They were calling us names and shouting, 'You're not camping here!' We said, 'We're only getting a drop of tea and we'll be shifting on when we collect the children.' But they wouldn't listen so we had to pack up and move on again.

Half of my lovely things got broken that time, my lovely china and glass. The guards and the Corporation can come and do this to a traveller but if we did the same to their houses we'd have to pay for it. We never got paid for the caravan they ruined. We had to manage in one caravan for all the children and the girls who weren't married.

On the rock on the shore is the cormorant's dwelling
The wild warbling blackbird has its nest in the tree
The birds of the air and the fish of the ocean
Each has its own place but there's no place for me.

The fox has its lair and the rabbit its burrow
The sett for the badger, the hive for the bee
The weasel, the hare, the mole and the marten
Each has its own shelter but there's no place for me.

We got it that hard being pushed around on the road that we moved into a site at Belcamp; it was for thirty-five or forty families and that was too many. I hated it. The huts were like paper. If there were children playing outside you could hear all the noise coming through the walls. The boys and girls had nothing to do, bar a few boys who had AnCO and they were the ones that didn't need it. The men were all just standing around with nothing to do, their way of life had gone.

My husband had a drink problem. He took the pledge for a year, but one day he went off with some settled men. About nine or ten o'clock at night the guards came and said, 'Your husband is down at the barracks, come down and bail him out.' When there's a gang of men together and they get drunk they don't want to leave the pub until it's closing time. The barman wanted him out because he was too drunk. They should have let him sit there but he was arrested. I hadn't the money for bail so I went round a few travellers, we always had this thing that if one was short they could collect from all.

My married daughter came down with me to the barracks, she was expecting a baby and I was sorry later for taking her. When I went in I said to the guard, 'Is he sobered up yet?' He said, 'I haven't been in for a long time — we're letting him sleep it off.' I said, 'Oh, great, he might be sobered now.' I don't look down on anyone who drinks because there's a reason for it. Good people can have a drink problem and my husband is a really good person. The guard said, 'We'll go in now and get him out.'

I was used to getting shocks but when they took my husband out of that cell I didn't really know him. He had no shirt on and he was completely covered with blood, even his trousers were stuck to his legs with blood. His head was slit wide open. My daughter nearly died with the fright she got; she is a nervous kind of girl, a quiet gentle person.

I asked all of the guards what happened but it was very peculiar none of them I asked was supposed to be in the barracks at the time. 'Sorry, missus, we weren't here, we're only after coming on duty,' more of them were going off duty. 'It must have been somebody did it,' I said. 'How would you like it if you got drunk and your wives had to come down and saw you in this state?'

We had to get him down to the hospital and get his head stitched and all the blood washed off before the children saw him. I would have forgiven the guards if they had taken him to hospital and then locked him up. But they just threw him in the cell and he drunk and bleeding. He could have died there and there would have been nothing about him because he was a traveller. I have found out through life that when you're a poor person from the slums or a traveller you don't matter. When I looked at my husband I thought of my father: maybe he died that way.

The chalets were really getting on my nerves so one day I went over to Clondalkin to stay with my daughter. She had two caravans so she was in one with her children and I slept in the other with my children. The next morning I was very sick and all my strength had gone. I was so run-down and tired I had the feeling I was finished.

When things get me down, ever since I was a child, I go off and pray on my own. You can really get in touch with God if you can concentrate, it's not like going to chapel where there are hundreds of people. My daughter brought me over a cup of tea and I was going to stay in bed but then I said to myself, 'I'll get up and say my prayers.'

It was raining a light rain so I put my coat around my shoulders and went outside. I was so tired, I could barely drag my feet, all my energy just seemed to go. I went through a gap into a big green field with high ditches where no-one could see me. I was completely alone and I could say my prayers. I blessed my face and I was praying but I felt so run down that I was crying at the one time. I was getting wet from the hazy rain but I didn't care about that. All of a sudden I got this burning on top of my head. I thought it was on fire. I put up my hand beside my forehead and I could feel the heat going through my fingers. I kept walking around but this burning wouldn't go away, it was like the sun on a hot summer's day.

There were two big trees in the field and I sat down under them on an old tree-stump because I felt so tired. I still kept saying my prayers. When I'm praying I have this habit of sort of talking to God at the one time. Of course I can't see him but I speak to him as though I can — I know he's there because I believe God is everywhere with us.

When I sat down the most peculiar thing happened. The largest bird I've ever seen came out from the top of the trees; it must have been nesting and maybe I disturbed it. It kept making an awful noise, flapping its wings. I got a terrible shock altogether and I didn't know whether to run out of the field or what. It wasn't really a natural bird like a pigeon or a crow or a pheasant, it was a big bluey-grey bird. When it was flapping its wings where I was sitting its feathers were falling down and some of them fell in my lap.

I hurried back to the gap and when I came to it I blessed my face — I was a bit shaky over the experience. When I crossed the gap the burning disappeared and when I put up my hand my hair was all wet from the rain.

The strange thing was that when I came outside the field I felt a different person: I felt brand-new. For days I hadn't even combed my hair or bathed the children and I hate to see them dirty because it looks miserable. When I went back over to the caravan I put on two pots of water on the gas and I gathered up the children and bathed them all and I put clean clothes inside and outside on them and I shampooed my own hair that I hadn't combed for days; I got this strength that I could go through anything and nothing could stop me.

I've had loads of experiences like this in my life — I suppose it happens to loads of people. I always pray to God, not just when I need something because I don't think you leave God till you need him, you need to thank him for the things you have. If you go to a hospital and look at the people there who are in bed for years and years you see that if you have problems yourself you still don't know how lucky you are — you can always be worse off.

We shifted out of Belcamp to Clondalkin, it was a mucky, terrible place. It's hard to get the children into school because they're tired of being pushed around and they're not really settling down but we got them going to the school at Neilstown. The teachers were all very good to the travelling children; mine were in with settled children and I think that was great. They should grow up together as children, not one as traveller and the other as settled, they should get the same education and the same rights, not make cheese of one and chalk of the other. In some of the schools they have classes just for the travelling children, they will be let out to play at one time and then the settled children will be let out at the other time. This is not really fair: the schools should be trying to break down the barriers, even Protestant and Catholic children should be in school together.

Mary and Ann, my two daughters that had the lead poisoning, had nervous breakdowns, the two of them together. Mary had lost her little girl a few years before. She and her husband didn't get on very well since they were married so they were separated and back again and separated again.

Mary and Ann were in a hospital a couple of miles from Clondalkin on the main Mullingar road. One night when I was going in to visit them and it was very dark and cold I met a lovely woman coming out of the hospital — the way you get to chatting someone if you see them crying. She had just left her husband and she was breaking her heart over him. I told her about my two daughters to try to make her feel better and she said, 'God help you, how can you stand it with two? It's an awful place.' Of course a nerve hospital is an awful place. 'I'll pray for you,' she said and I showed her where to get the bus. I went in to see my daughters and when I came out she was gone.

The heather will fade and the bracken will die
Streams will run cold and clear
And the small birds will be going
And it's then you'll be knowing
That the terror time is near.

We stayed in Clondalkin for a few months and we were getting on well there because none of the settled people ever bothered us — we weren't really beside them. The big snow came and some of the travellers had an awful time. The windows were broken in some of the caravans. One woman told me that when she got up in the middle of the night the whole caravan was full of snow and the children were all screaming with the cold because the snow was on their bed. When I was going to see my daughters one day I saw little children walking in the snow and their feet were swollen up — they had no shoes on them. They were living in an old caravan with no doors and they were all crying — it was curelty. There was hay thrown to sheep and feed for cows but no-one came to see if the travellers were dead or alive. They hadn't even got water — they had to walk miles with prams and wheels to get it. We were able to look after ourselves, we had the generator and a gas heater but there were caravans with nothing at all. If settled people knew the way some of the travellers live they wouldn't be as hard on them. If they went in to see them and chat them they'd learn that they're people like themselves.

11.

The chance to speak out

There was talk about the travellers being moved from Clondalkin. Bulldozers came, dug up the muck and built it up about six feet high along the road for miles; this was to stop travellers pulling in. We shifted over to Tallaght and camped at the crossroads, at the Protestant church beside a graveyard. It was a lovely place and we used to try and keep it tidy but when you have no bin collection the dirt piles up.

Years ago the travellers only stayed in small groups because you could pull the wagon in anywhere, there was no traffic and there were plenty of camps. We had baskets for food and cans for milk so there were no boxes and plastic bags and bottles from supermarkets for rubbish. Today you have the travellers all piled in on top of one another because their favourite places for camping have been done away with or built on. That's what happened in Tallaght; travellers don't want to live like that but they have nowhere else to go.

Farewell to the besoms of heather and broom
Farewell to the creel and the basket
The folks of today they would far sooner pay
For a thing that's made out of plastic.

Farewell to the pony, the cob and the mare
The reins and the harness are idle
You don't need the strap when you're breaking up scrap
So farewell to the bit and the bridle.

Whatever is wrong today the people are being set against each other. They're building houses for settled people where there are no amenities for them and then when they're working they have so much tax to pay and so much taken off them it sets them against the unemployed — they say, 'You're living off the land.' The people are so tormented that when the travellers camp beside them they sort of knock it out of them. They should be knocking it out of the government or the county councillors because the travellers have suffered enough down through the years.

There were about seven or eight families in the field where we were camping. We all had our little bit of privacy because we weren't on top of one another. In one corner was a family group with the granny and the grandchildren and the old uncles. The old men had a couple of horses and you couldn't expect them to give up their horses — you might as well cut their heads off because their horses are all they have left of their tradition and their life.

There was another family group in another corner and then there was us with my married daughters and sons-in-law. We were trying to get skips for the rubbish. I got my children into school in Tallaght — I don't know how many schools they were at! — and they were getting on great because they were growing up with the settled children and nobody called them knackers.

Then a crowd of settled people decided they wanted to get the travellers out of Tallaght.

Some of them came up — ordinary people not guards — and give us forty-eight hours to get out. It was like something from a cowboy movie; and yet this was Ireland, a Catholic country, a great Christian country for years and years. It was very hard to believe that people would come and do this, walking up to every caravan and some of the poor women were barely surviving trying to live and to cope with the little children. They said if we didn't leave they'd march on us.

We wouldn't go in the forty-eight hours so there was a big march against us. Some of the children were very nervous. My little boy Richard wouldn't go to school, he was saying, 'Mammy, what about all the people — they'll kill me down the road then I come out.' This is the way the travelling children are growing up: in fear of everything and it's not right because it'll turn them into hardened criminals or into nervous wrecks — afraid of everything and never able to speak out for themselves. If you grow up in fear it's only the very odd person that will speak out.

I tried to explain to Richard that the people were marching and that they wouldn't do any violence, and they didn't.

Father Vincent Travers came down to see if we were all right and he gave us comfort. He's what I call a really good priest, a priest that'll speak out. He stood on our side but he wasn't against the settled people: if they'd been in the state we were in he would have sided with them.

When the march came down there was a lot of chanting like the Ku Klux Klan, they were all shouting 'Out, out, out,' all together. Some of the travelling women were very nervous, and some of them weren't and the men weren't they were just tired of moving and moving and being afeared.

Just as the march was beginning some settled people came down from Tallaght and stood with us. That's something that never happened before in all the places I have been where people came against travellers. It's very hard for settled people to stand with travellers because they'll be called 'knacker-lovers' and they have to live with settled people whereas we're a bit out from them. These were ordinary people, housewives and working men who all had their own families and their own houses in Tallaght that they were trying to buy. And they weren't bitter people, they were standing on the side of justice for a small group. I thought it was great of them to stand with us and give us some sort of hope.

After the big march Gay Byrne came out and did his morning show with us, outside in the field. So many people came the place was full of them; they were all on top of the travellers and walking around the fires where some of the old men were making a drop of tea. If you walked in on settled people, into their privacy and trampled their gardens there'd be a big kick-up about it but these people were just standing around as if we were dirt — as if we didn't matter but they mattered, as if we weren't people but they were people.

I got the chance to speak on Gay Byrne's programme about all the things that had been going on and the names the travellers were being called. It's very easy to call people names if they can't speak back — it's like going up and battering a little child. Speaking to the travellers at that time was like speaking to children because they never got the chance to speak back. I read the papers a lot and sometimes I was glad that some of the travellers didn't read, the way they couldn't hear the things that were said about them for if they did they would go mad. When you read and see what's going on it really torments you.

Father Travers came down to see us and I was telling him the way travellers were treated and all the terrible things that are said about us and how we don't get a chance to speak up for ourselves. I wrote a travellers' manifesto — what we should have and our needs. Father Travers typed it for me and he drove me round and we dropped letters in to all the newspapers. From then on the travellers' names were mentioned and mentioned in the papers and on radio and television and it wasn't all bad; before we went to Tallaght the things you heard about the travellers were all bad. I wouldn't wonder for the settled people to be against us because they were hearing nothing but bad about us and they thought we were all the same and we're not. There's only a tiny few of the travellers committing crime. Some of the travellers are really good people, they don't break the law and they're just trying to survive.

A group of us got together after the march to work for travellers' rights. There were settled people from Tallaght: Tony Hackett and his wife Marie, Seamus Leonard, a night porter in a hospital down town, Mervyn Ennis a community worker and Willie Power who worked in a supermarket. Then there was myself and my husband John and Michael McCann and his brothers and later on my sister Chrissie Ward and her husband Paddy and my brother Peter Donoghue and his wife Kathleen joined in.

At first we held the meetings at the caravans. It was the summertime and we'd gather outside every Sunday but it was very hard to get the travellers to come. When people have been walked on for years and pushed aside and treated as dirt, they feel they are dirt. The way they were treated by everyone, even the Catholic Church they felt they weren't even human beings.

We got a little place in Tallaght in a schoolroom where we could have a meeting every week. Then the travellers sort of stopped coming when they saw nothing being done. The Corporation and the County Council and the government could only do so much; they could try to get us proper places to live in and it wouldn't be begging for charity, it would be our right to have those places and we'd be paying rent for them. But

Travelling in style through
O'Connell Street during a
Minceir Misli protest in 1984

The travellers are
attracting support
from many concerned groups
in the settled community. Here,
a Family Aid supporter walks in
a Minceir Misli march in Dublin

The Tallaght bypass

My husband John
leading a protest
through Tallaght following
the arrest of some travellers

An anti-traveller demonstration in Tallaght

Some of the courageous settled people who supported the travellers in Tallaght

DEREK SPEIRS (REPORT)

Listening to the speeches at the GPO during a Minceir Misli rally in July 1984 if the settled people didn't allow sites nothing was ever going to be done, they were the most important for us to get to. Someone had to go out and break down the barriers. So we started the Travellers' Rights Committee; it was just a little pressure group. We got invited to meetings all around the country. I went around schools, convents and colleges giving talks about the culture of the travellers and the way we're treated because it's been hidden for years. In Ireland we're so good to foreigners and it is good to help anyone who doesn't get the chance to speak for themselves. But I felt that we'd been put under the mat and forgotten about. There was always a big queue and we were at the end of it and when we came the doors were always closed and we got nothing.

When you go to speak to a lot of young people you think they're going to be noisy but everywhere I went the students just sat listening, there wasn't a sound out of them.

I remember speaking to over three hundred girls at a school in Milltown. I was well used to speaking to girls because I have seven of my own. They were really interested but you can't keep speaking serious to teenagers and children because they get a bit bored so I was throwing in little funny things so they could have a laugh as well. Some of the girls were sitting on the floor and when I was done speaking they all flocked around me and they were asking how they could help. This was a great start, getting to the young people. The teachers came over and I said, 'They were so quiet, there wasn't a sound out of them.' And the teachers said, 'You should be in class in the morning and you'd hear them and you'd know if they were quiet or not!'

When I went down to Waterford with some of the committee to give a talk I thought the people were going to be hostile but I was treated like a queen — I couldn't really believe it. People were getting up and reading letters to me and saying I was this and I was that: I'm just an ordinary woman but the welcome we got was great. Before we go to a meeting in a new place we always make a point of speaking to some of the travellers who are living there. We have to be able to speak about what they would want for they mightn't like what we'd like.

Then we were invited to Cork, to the college there. The students were great; they got us all places to stay and after the meeting we sat up until about three o'clock with them singing and chatting. The students were very jolly, they were singing 'The banks of my own lovely Lee' and I was singing for them too. Next morning they brought us around and showed us Cork. We went to a wild-life park. It had a big lake with an island in the middle with bushes and every kind of bird you could mention and there were hundreds of swans. There was one black swan among them and I said, 'That's me there!'

Some of the students — and they were Irish — knew nothing about the travellers, it was as if we'd come from the moon. The questions they asked! 'Do you marry?' They didn't know if we got married or if we lived together, if we had the children on the roadside or if we went to hospital. It was like speaking of something from out of the world. They could tell you the history of the North American Indians but here were the Irish travellers in their own country and they could tell you nothing about them, their history or their traditions. And these are the people who'll be running the country when we're all gone.

The thing I remarked, going around, was that there never was one traveller boy or girl going through college. Students from all over the world came to Ireland but it really hurt me that in this day and age there never was one traveller boy or girl among the students listening to me.

I loved going around speaking to people who didn't know anything about the travellers. Some of them were really against us and if I got through to one or two of them it was a great day's work. There was even a priest who came up to see me and he admitted that he never went into a travellers' camp in his life. He said 'Nan, I often passed them but I never went in to them.' Here was a priest, and he must have been thirty years of age, who never went in to sit with the travellers and they Christian people. I gave him a great chat. I told him the travellers were forgotten about by the Catholic Church and I wonder today how it is they still have their deep faith in God.

A few weeks later I saw the priest again and he said, 'Nan, you know when I went home that evening I went to bed and I couldn't sleep I felt so guilty.' I thought it was really brave of him and great of him to say it. 'I kept thinking of what you were saying to me,' he said, 'and it was running through my head.' Next day he went round the travellers and chatted them. And he said he'd missed so much by not talking to them before.

In the summer we did so many pickets and marches on the Dáil there must be a hole outside Leinster House! When we thought people were tired of looking at marches we decided to do something different to catch attention. We drove the pony and cart up to the Dáil. The guards on duty were really nice, they didn't stop us bringing the horse in and they came over and chatted us. I spoke on the microphone and we gave out leaflets. We gave out leaflets at every march and the tourists here on holidays took them back to their own countries.

People started coming to see me out at the caravan, they were coming from everywhere — America, China, India, Africa.... There were Joyces from America coming all roads: 'We're the Joyces that went to America and done well and ye're the ones that stayed at home!' And I said, 'Yes, we're still living in the Stone Age.' There were people coming at all hours, they'd come with cameras and they'd say, 'Mrs Joyce, can we have our photos taken with you at the caravan?' I don't know how many photos of us there must be over there — they must be all over America! I was getting tormented with these people because when my husband wouldn't get his tea he would get real contrary.

A general election was called for late 1982. We weren't expecting it but we decided that I should be a candidate — to get publicity for travellers' rights. I felt like Daniel going into the lion's den, that I was going to be eaten up! I'm sure some people were shocked at a traveller going up for election and there was some hostility but we got loads of offers of help from settled people in Tallaght, students and women's groups. There were thousands of letters to be sent out and leaflets and posters but the committee worked very hard and I went around speaking and to meetings. I remember some settled women from Tallaght coming up to me and saying, 'Your poster looks better than Mr Haughey's — we're sick of looking at him!'

A crew from the BBC came out to the caravan one morning to do a programme on me, it was to be shown after the election. They were all freezing so they came in to the caravan and the girls made a big kettle of tea for them. They wanted to film me campaigning down at the supermarket so we went down and I was going around giving out leaflets and speaking. I had a little microphone inside my coat, the television people were in the van and no-one knew there was a camera on them. Some of the women were coming over and shaking hands with me and more of them were putting their arms round me and they were saying, 'Mrs Joyce, we'd give you our number one but we're giving it to Mervyn Taylor but we'll give you our number two.' And they were saying, 'You're a very brave woman, you're great.' But other women were calling me terrible names, calling the travellers dirt and filth and saying we should be done away with. I was well used to this, it didn't get me down. I felt sorry for them not myself; I could have said things to them but I wouldn't go down to their level. I don't think you get anywhere by calling people names, it's really not right.

One woman said to me, 'The travellers should be burned'; this was a Christian woman, that goes to Mass on Sunday, a good Catholic. The things she was coming out with! She was being filmed the whole time and recorded and she didn't know it. Now you can't put people on television unless they're willing so she had to be told she'd been filmed. She nearly died! 'Don't you put that on television, no, no, no!' It just shows you the way people will say things but they won't come out into the open with them.

But then people can change too. When I was going round at the polling station the day of the election an old man came up to me: he was one of the men who gave us forty-eight hours to leave Tallaght. He had turned into a completely different person. 'We want you to come and live with us,' he said, 'and we want you to have your rights.' He was a lovely person.

The election gave me a great chance to say all the things that had been boiling up inside me for years and years — nothing like it had ever happened before for the travellers. I got five hundred and eighty votes* and I thought it was great. I couldn't promise people anything for their vote so by voting for me they got nothing. But they were voting for human rights and justice and this was a great start.

---

*This was as many first preferences as the two community candidates put together.

14

Arrest

ITINERANT ON CHARGE OF JEWEL THEFT
... Mrs Nan Joyce, who stood as candidate in the last general election in the cause of travelling people, appeared in the Dublin District Court yesterday charged with stealing almost £3,500 worth of jewellery.... [and] with receiving a gold bangle valued at £120.

Irish Press 8 June 1983

The police started harassing us; for months they were coming from all over Dublin to search the caravan and turn everything upside down; they would find nothing because there was nothing to find.

There were two bus-stops where we were staying, one at each side of the road. In the evenings the buses would be full of workmen and people going home and they would pull up right at the door of the caravan with all those guards and squad cars around. I was saying to myself, 'What will the people think if they see all those guards here every day?' I was really worried about it because the committee had been at it for so long and we'd worked so hard. I had got people to know me and trust me as a speaker for the travellers and here were the guards around the place.

I woke up suddenly one morning and saw a crowd of strange men in the trailer. They just rushed in the door, three or four of them in plain clothes, and a *ban garda*,[11] and hs was so ignorant she wouldn't even speak to me, she was pulling everything out of the presses. I said, 'Are you not supposed to knock before you come in to someone's place?'and I asked them what they were looking for. One of them said, 'We're looking for jewellery.'

I have two rings and a gold chain and a pair of gold sovereign earrings that I bought years ago — travellers love things like that. I keep them in my handbag because when you have little grandchildren they're always at the drawers and they pull out things and lose them. I had my bag under my pillow so I took it out and opened it and spread my things out on the bed — I was trying to keep myself covered with the sheets at the one time. 'There,' I said, 'that's all the jewellery I have.' They never even looked at it! This is how I know they weren't looking for jewellery.

The same guards and *ban garda* came back next morning while I was trying to get the children ready for school. They turned everything upside-down and they took a bracelet from a drawer full of junk. Then they said they were arresting me and pulled me out the door. I said, 'Could you leave me send the children off to school before they see me going in a squad car? I have them all ready, just let me put them out the door and they'll run on to school.' But they caught me by the arm and pulled me out.

It was about twenty to nine in the morning and I had no coat on, just an old skirt and blouse and mucky boots because you can't wear shoes around the fields when it's raining, they stick in the mud. My hair was just up with two clips on top of my head because when I get up in the morning I just wash my hands to cook the breakfast, I don't wash my face or comb my hair until later on. It nearly killed me altogether to be brought off like this.

They brought me on to a police barrack, I think it was Crumlin but I'm not quite sure, and I was in an awful state, I didn't know what was going on. They threw me into a cell and there was a smell off it would knock you down because whoever had been in it before me had used the toilet and wasn't able to flush it because the chain was outside. After a bit one of the guards from outside pulled the chain so it wasn't too bad then.

The cell was tiny and there was blood on the walls. I was in there for a couple of hours but I thought it was for a lifetime because I have a phobia and when I'm in a closed-in space I feel all the walls coming in on me, I feel as if I'm smothering. Every minute I'd go over to the hole in the door to get air — it was as if I was drowning. I just kept marching up and down, I couldn't sit easy.

When I was locked in that dark cell the first thing I thought of was my father, what he must have felt like when he died in prison on his own.

I've had a lot of bad experiences in my life but this was the worst I ever had. Everything kept running into my head and when I heard the bolts going across the door I got sick. I kept throwing up though I had no breakfast that morning because they didn't give me time to get it.

After about two hours they took me out of the cell and I was as sick as anything, I could feel my face, really cold. A young *ban garda* was just after coming on duty — the one before her was so ignorant she wouldn't even speak to me — and she was a really lovely person. I felt so terrible I asked her could I wash my face and hands. She said, 'Sorry, Mrs Joyce, we don't have much facilities for women, but I'll take you in,' and she brought me in to the washroom. There was a big large towel hanging up and when I went to dry my hands I saw blood running off it on to the floor, the towel was wringing wet with blood. I nearly died, my nerves went completely. I said to the *ban garda*, 'What in the name of God is on the towel?' She sort of pulled me away and gave me something else to dry my hands with.

When I came out the guard had this statement all ready — he must have done it when I was in the cell because he didn't do it when I was speaking to him. He said, 'We're charging you with stealing £500 worth of jewellery and with receiving a gold bangle.' I nearly died with the shock, I thought he was only codding at first to frighten me. I said, 'Go away, you're only joking.' He said, 'You're going down to court.'

It was after some holiday so the court was packed. Before you come up to be tried you're waiting in a sort of a tunnel downstairs with cells on it. My nerves just went; I felt terrible. They didn't let me bring my bag or my cigarettes and then to have no coat and the mucky boots and my hair not combed I felt awful to be coming into the court like this because I always like to keep myself tidy especially if I'm going anywhere.

I was in a panic waiting downstairs. The young *ban garda* was still with me and she was sitting beside me on the bench. She kept chatting me, and she told me where she was from and she said, 'Don't worry now, it'll all be straightened out, you'll be all right in a few minutes.' I was dying for a cigarette for I'm a heavy smoker and it would have cooled my nerves. The ban garda went off and begged a guard for a cigarette and a light, it was really great of her and I'd rather have had that cigarette than ten thousand pounds! Some of the guards knew me from the papers and they were really nice to me.

While we were waiting we heard all this shouting upstairs, and I said to the *ban garda*, 'In the name of God who's shouting up there? Is that where I have to go?' When I went up I saw it was Mr Ó hUadhaigh, the judge, who was shouting. He was a very fair man in his ways and he was a great judge because you didn't feel as much afeared of him as you would of a straight-faced, real serious judge. Sometimes he'd say things and you'd laugh but you weren't laughing at him it was just his funny sayings, I use words in the same way.

The guard said I was from Tallaght. Mr Ó hUadhaigh looked at me and I suppose he took pity on me because he said, 'This woman has eleven children.'

> Asked by Justice Ó hUadhaigh if she wanted free legal aid Mrs Joyce refused and said 'I don't want anything for free — I'm well able to speak for myself.' 'I know you are,' the Justice replied, 'I've seen you on television.' Mrs Joyce was remanded on bail until 14 June.
>
> *Irish Press* 8 June 1983

The guards had no book of evidence ready so I got out on bail but I had to go back again and again. I was a nervous wreck, I couldn't sleep at night and I lost an awful lot of weight. The day after I was arrested a travelling man gave me the paper and he said, 'Nan, your name is on the paper that you're up for so much jewellery. I never knew that you'd steal anything!' And people that knew me, that were really my friends were coming out with jokes, calling me 'cat burglar' and things like that. But it wasn't a joke to me. I felt so down I just kept in the caravan I didn't want to go out and face anyone, I'd break down when I'd think about it.

One day I went down the town, I'm great friends with the women in the markets. One woman said, 'Hello, Mrs Joyce, how are you?' When the woman beside her heard I was Mrs Joyce she moved her handbag, I could see her catching on to her bag and it nearly killed me, just looking at her. For a few days after, I wouldn't come out of the caravan, I was afeared to go out and face the people in case they'd say, 'Oh, there's the one that was speaking up for the travellers — when she'd do this, what would the rest of them do?'

People had come to know me and trust me and now I felt everything was gone. I'd say to myself, 'When I'm speaking to people again what will they be thinking, they won't believe me.'

Then settled people came along and they were saying 'Mrs Joyce, you needn't worry, we don't believe you'd ever do anything like that.' That was a great help. Some women that I'd never met came up the whole way from Cork to give me their support. They said they didn't believe it and that something should be done about arresting people in the wrong. They took me out for an evening to give my mind a rest. Father Travers came up to give me courage and so did Father Mernagh and Father McCullough and they were all really great.

About a week after I was arrested I was in court again and the charge of stealing was dropped but I still had to go back over the receiving charge, over a bracelet one of the children found. We have old scrap cars for selling for parts and when one is brought in the little boys go out and lift up the seats. They find loose change or old biros or keys — various things like that. One morning they came in with a bracelet and a load of old tapes and combs but I was real busy, I was scrubbing the floor. 'Throw out that old rubbish,' I said, 'I've enough in here.' Patrick gave the bracelet to his little sister and I completely forgot about it. This was the bracelet they were on about! I had to keep going back to court for months and months, and in the end after all the waiting and nervous strain, that charge was dropped too.

I felt really down about the whole thing but then I said to myself, 'If I give up, if I don't go on speaking out, people will think I was guilty.'

Father Mernagh said I should go to a seminar that Trócaire was holding in Galway — there were bishops from all over the world going to it. This was a week or so after I was arrested. We sat down and we thought how we'd get into the seminar — it was like breaking into a prison! There were workshops on different things and Father Mernagh got us places in the one on human rights. He went along and myself and Mervyn Ennis. There were people there from around the world with so much to say, people working for various charities, nuns and priests from foreign countries where poor people are being badly treated. Sean MacBride was in our workshop and so was Michael D. Higgins. We all got a chance to speak and it was just great.

The chairman from each workshop was to get up at the seminar in front of those hundreds of people and say what they'd been speaking about. Our workshop voted for me to speak and I was very grateful for the chance. We were supposed to speak for five minutes but I went on and on I said I thought it was great to help foreign countries and the poor hungry children of the world and the outcasts but first we should look at our own doorstep and do something about our own people.

> The Trócaire seminar was reminded that the travelling people in Ireland need attention as urgently as the poor of the developing countries. 'We are treated as outcasts in our own country,' Mrs Nan Joyce said. 'You people are very concerned about the Third World. I think you should also be concerned about us, we are the Fourth World. We live among rats in camps or caravans . . . our children suffer from as many diseases as the children of the Third World.' Mrs Joyce had an extraordinary impact on the seminar, receiving more applause than anyone else who presented reports.
>
> *The Irish Times* 18 June 1983

Here was I after crashing into this big place with all those highly educated people and cardinals and bishops from all over the world. I'm sure there were people angry over what I said to them but it doesn't matter how well educated you are you have to be told. I find that some educated people are very ignorant of the facts; they come out and tell you to do this and why don't you do that and they know nothing at all about it. And then you get foreigners coming and writing books about us: some of those books are very hurtful — the people who wrote them should be sued.

13.

A better understanding

When I was a child I remember going hawking the houses one day with my mother. It was freezing cold and people kept banging the doors in our faces. If anyone gave something they wouldn't speak to us: we weren't real people to them.

The door of the chapel was always open so we went in and my mother lit a candle. As she was down on her knees praying with the child in her arms, I looked at the statue of Our Lady with the Child Jesus in a sort of a shawl. I looked at my mother and I wondered why people should be treated like this and I said to myself, 'I'll make a better life when I grow up — I won't have to beg, I won't have to be pitiful-looking to get charity just to survive.'

Well, I wonder sometimes did I make a better life. I never really wanted anything for myself but I wanted things for the children, a warm place for them in the winter and a clean bed and enough food. My older children got no education, they lost out on everything because we were hunted from place to place. Young people are completely lost today if they can't read or write, they can't manage computers or anything and their traditional way of life is gone.

My two youngest children got a better chance: they started school at the right age with the settled children and they're getting on great. I'd like to be able to afford to send them to college. But they will still always be travellers. I would like all the travelling children to have self-confidence and to grow up proud of what they are because they are very special people with their own traditions and their own way of life. But the way they've been treated and discriminated against they grow up ashamed of their own parents.

It used to be that the one time you heard about travellers was when they did wrong; nothing about us was ever taught in schools and when children came by our camp they would just run by — they were afeared of the travellers. Even today some people are afeared to come near us and chat with us — it's a fear of the unknown.

But the last few years have been a great point in the travellers' history. When I first started speaking it was very hard to get other travellers to speak as well or to take my place the day I wouldn't get out but now there are loads of travellers well able and willing to speak up for themselves. Our own group, Mincéir Misli, is working for travellers rights and we have help from settled people and priests and nuns who want us to help oursleves — not to be doing things for us — and that's another great change. And today the newspapers and the radio and television are very fair to us.

We are a different people. There'll always be travellers who want to keep going when they see the summer and they feel lonely. If I'm in the one camp now I'll sort of get tired and I'll move the trailer up about thirty yards and I'll feel that I'm after shifting. We shouldn't be bullied to settle down. I would love a house in the wintertime but I'd like to be free to go off if I took it into my head maybe to go to Belfast for a couple of months.

We are a different people but what we want most of all is a better understanding with the settled people: that we should understand them and that they should understand us — the travelling people.

NOTES

1. *Free State*, the Republic of Ireland
2. *A grá*, my love
3. *céilí*, a dance
4. *bodhrán*, musical instrument
5. *to be ignorant*, used in the sense of being ill-mannered
6. *a garsún*, my boy
7. *forenenst*, in front of
8. *guard*, policeman — from the Irish *Garda Síochána*, Guardians of the Peace
9. *Late Late Show*, very popular live television programme presented by Gay Byrne who also hosts a morning radio programme
10. *Stardust*, a nightclub, the scene of a tragedy on St Valentine's Night 1981 when 48 young people died in a fire
11. *ban garda*, woman police officer

This is the personal story of Nan Joyce, traveller. It is the story of a girl born into poverty and orphaned in her early teens who has developed into a proud and independent spokesperson for her people.

She tells the story of her own family, of idyllic days camped near Downpatrick, of the beauty of the countryside, of horsefairs and marriage customs, campfire gatherings and story-telling and of hardships endured especially during the terrible year her father died. Nearly destitute, her mother went out to steal scrap, was caught and sent to prison. Nan and her brothers and sisters were left to survive alone.

In recent years a vigorous campaign for travellers' rights has been developed in which Nan Joyce has played a leading part. Her voice has been the most prominent and articulate among those who have demanded justice for the travelling people. She has stood as a candidate in one general election and has made numerous radio and television appearances.

TRAVELLER is a moving personal document, and the authentic voice of a submerged community. Nan Joyce's courage and humour stand as a remarkable affirmation of human dignity in adversity.

ANNA FARMAR is Communications Officer for Self Help, the organisation for Third World self help development. She has worked for many years as a freelance editor.

Cover design by Noel Lewis
Photograph of Nan Joyce by Derek Spiers
Photograph of campsite courtesy of The Irish Times
7171 1388 4

Gill and Macmillan